Routledge Revivals

Deceleration in the Eighteenth-Century British Economy

Originally published in 1976 the theme of this book was that the advance of the British economy between 1660 and 1780 was not continuous and, contrary to a widely held view, there was a pause or at best retarded growth between about 1725 and 1750. Substantiated by reference to the development of a number of industries and regions, the author argues that labour's attitude to work, demographic change and government policies militated against growth. The main argument challenges the view that the second quarter of the eighteenth century witnessed general and sustained economic growth and development. It is argued that low food prices did not generate as much additional purchasing power among the labouring people as some historians have maintained. Nor was most of the additional purchasing power used in ways which promoted the development of the British economy. This deceleration theory is a key point of debate in economic history, and this book is a valuable contribution to this debate.

Deceleration in the Eighteenth-Century British Economy

Anthony J. Little

Routledge
Taylor & Francis Group
Routledge Revivals

First published in 1976 by Croom Helm Ltd.

This edition first published in 2026 by Routledge
4 Park Square, Milton Park, Abingdon, Oxon, OX14 4RN

and by Routledge
605 Third Avenue, New York, NY 10158

Routledge is an imprint of the Taylor & Francis Group, an informa business

ISBN: 978-1-041-27923-5 (hbk)
ISBN: 978-1-003-75692-7 (ebk)
ISBN: 978-1-041-27926-6 (pbk)

Book DOI 10.4324/9781003756927

Deceleration in the Eighteenth-Century British Economy

Anthony J Little

Croom Helm London

First published 1976

Croom Helm Ltd, 2–10 St John's Road, London SW11

ISBN 0–85664–340–8

Printed in Great Britain
by Redwood Burn Ltd, Trowbridge and Esher

CONTENTS

PREFACE

This small book is concerned with some major economic features, trends and developments in pre-industrial Britain. Attention is focused on the period preceding the Industrial Revolution. It is contended that the forces making for economic progress in the seventeenth and early eighteenth centuries, especially after 1660, weakened in the 1720s, and that the second quarter of the eighteenth century witnessed comparative stagnation. The vigorous expansion over 1750–80 leading into the factory age is so well known that only brief references are made to these decades.

The topic is a controversial one. Views expressed will be opposed, probably by those who see little economic development between 1660 and 1750, and certainly by those who see sustained and perhaps accelerating growth over the whole of this period. The main argument is that low food prices in the 1730s and 1740s did not generate considerable additional purchasing power, nor does it seem likely that the pattern of increased spending promoted economic development. These conclusions are borne out by the experience of many industries and regions. It also appears that labour's attitude to work, demographic change, and government economic policies all militated against growth.

The book is very largely a survey of some of the literature which bears on the topic. No more ambitious claim is made for it than this. The work is based almost exclusively on secondary sources, and hence will be unsuitable for readers who believe history can be written only by those who at least sometimes bury themselves in museums and archives. Readers who have little or no knowledge of the period under review should have no difficulty in following the text. In a few places, and they are few, acquaintance with elementary economic terminology will be helpful.

The extent of my indebtedness to so many writers is inadequately reflected in footnote references and the bibliography. I have tried, though I am sure without complete success, to acknowledge the source of all material. I apologize to writers to whom I have unintentionally failed to give proper acknowledgement. For allowing me to quote at some length from their work, I wish to thank Professor D.C. Coleman, Professor A.H. John, and Professor Peter Mathias. I also thank Miss Deane and Cambridge University Press for permission to quote liberally from *The First Industrial Revolution.* I am grateful to everyone who has written to me, and especially to Dr. L.A. Clarkson, Professor A.W. Coats, Professor Ralph Davis, and Professor G.E. Mingay for their consent to publish extracts for their correspondence. I have received many useful comments not only from the latter but also from Dr. S.D. Chapman, Professor John, and Dr. A.G. Kenwood. I alone am responsible for any remaining mistakes and misconceptions. And I should add that none of the above is necessarily committed to the general theme of the book. Indeed, I am sorry to report that Professor John refuses to be converted.

I can always plead extenuating circumstances. In the first place, I was tempted to undertake the work by David Chambers. I was further aided and abetted by Bob Coats and Gordon Mingay. Perhaps they should have known better. In apportioning the balme, I am sure Gordon Mingay bears the greatest responsibility. Finally, I am grateful to my wife for typing all the drafts, and to David Jones for preparing the index.

A.J. Little
University of Queensland
Brisbane

1 THE PROBLEM AND ITS HISTORICAL CONTEXT

. . . it is difficult to resist the conclusion that such progress as occurred was a feature of the seventeenth century rather than of the sixteenth – and of the later seventeenth century rather than of the earlier.
(F.J. Fisher)

Such was the general pattern of regional economic change in the first three-quarters of the eighteenth century: an acceleration of expansion in industry, transport, agriculture, and inland trade, to the early 1720s; a falling off in the rate of expansion in all these branches until the 1740s, followed by an upward movement on all sides on such a scale as to presage the advent of a new age. (J. D. Chambers)[1]

Introduction

Economic historians have long debated the origins of the Industrial Revolution and the mechanics of growth in pre-industrial Britain. There is a large measure of agreement that the Industrial Revolution dates from the 1780s when the rate of increase of manufactured output rose sharply. But the reasons for this "take-off" are still controversial. Even the terminology has been a cause for concern as some historians have stressed the evolutionary nature of British economic development in and before the eighteenth century. We share the view of many writers who regard the transformation of the British economy (and way of life) between about 1780 and 1850 as revolutionary, but who also see a very long evolutionary process which somehow culminated in the Industrial Revolution.

A major difficulty when dealing with pre-industrial Britain is how to assess economic progress. If we follow modern economists and adopt increases in output or real income per head as a measure of growth, then we should have to conclude that development was pitifully slow. In our opinion, such an approach is unhelpful. An increase in output per head might be temporary and have no significant lasting implications for the economy. Far more important were changes which, in some sense, paved the way for long-term alterations in the structure of the economy.

We must guard against overvaluing increases in output which constituted extensive growth – i.e. more of the same – within the framework of traditional arrangements and production techniques. And we must be ready to tolerate drawn-out gestation periods in considering development in pre-industrial Britain. Furthermore, an important aspect of economic progress was the removal of impediments to growth or bottlenecks, especially in industries which were destined to become dominant in the Industrial Revolution.

In what follows we shall be concerned with some of the chief economic trends and milestones leading to the Industrial Revolution. Particular attention will be paid to the period after the Restoration. We believe that British economic history between 1660 and 1780 consists of three phases, two of vigorous development and one of deceleration or comparative stagnation. There is a consensus that the tempo of economic advance quickened during the three decades before about 1780. Again, there is general, though not universal, agreement that expansion occurred in a number of significant directions after 1660. Many historians see a continuous and perhaps an accelerating advance of the British economy from the late seventeenth century. By contrast with this view, we shall argue that the forces making for growth after 1660 weakened in the early eighteenth century, and the period from about 1725 to 1750 witnessed a check, a pause, or at best retarded economic advance. However, before we set out the problem, it might be useful to some readers if the period under review was placed in its historical context.

Agriculture

The output of pre-industrial Britain consisted overwhelmingly of farm products and the production of industries drawing their raw materials from the agricultural sector. The predominance of agriculture was evidenced in expenditure patterns. Thus it has been estimated that, towards the end of the seventeenth century, almost half of national expenditure was devoted to food (especially coarse-grain bread) and drink (especially beer), and perhaps a quarter to clothing (especially wool textiles). The productivity of agriculture was low. In average or good years, food production, particularly when supplemented with game and fish, was sufficient to provide a modest, though usually monotonous, diet for the bulk of the population. In less than average or bad years, hung hunger was widespread and some might have faced starvation. Historians disagree in their assessment of agricultural progress before 1750/60 Dr. Kerridge's enthusiasm is almost boundless as he assures us: "Early modern English farmers were bursting with industry and enterprise." But Professor Pawson sees them in a different light:

> Agriculture has made little progress in increased production for many centuries. It is recorded that in the seventeenth century one half of the country was covered by forest, moorland, and bog. The methods of farming reflected the influence of the Roman occupation and, indeed, in many respects were not unlike those described by Virgil 1,700 years earlier.[2]

It is likely that the truth lies between these extreme views, that agriculture was generally backward before the second half of the eighteenth century, but progress occurred in some regions during the sixteenth, seventeenth, and early eighteenth centuries.

Why was agricultural productivity low in many parts of the country? A major obstacle to farming improvement was the widespread open-field common-right system under which more than half the output of grains was grown. The following features of the system are especially relevant. An individual holding, or farm, consisted of a number of scattered strips in the open fields. Communal decisions taken at the manorial court or village meeting were made with regard to manuring, ploughing, sowing and harvesting. Co-operative effort sometimes extended to the pooling of seed and manure, and to the loaning of horses or oxen for the village plough-team. Many villagers had customary rights to the common land – i.e. the waste, uncultivated land. For example, they ran livestock on this land, collected wood and peat in the nearby forest, hunted there and fished in the local stream or river.

Under these arrangements, land, labour and materials were wasted. Each open field was usually left fallow every third year. Paths or furrows separated the strips, and so even more land was unproductive. Because each farmer's strips were scattered, he had unnecessarily long journeys to make, and of course some of the seed, manure and fertilizer he carried were inevitably lost. Manure was also wasted because livestock were allowed to wander over large stretches of common land. Again, labour was wasted in providing what has been called "human fences to the corn and meadows". Systematic work and the proper supervision of labourers were difficult or impossible. If a farmer chose to sow later than his neighbours, he probably harmed their sprouting seedlings; a farmer who harvested late delayed the use of land for common grazing. Unlimited grazing rights often led to the overstocking of commons, and scientific breeding was impossible where livestock were herded indiscriminately together.

During the seventeenth century, some writers on agriculture and progressive farmers and landowners became increasingly aware of the main obstacles to agricultural advance. Although the open-field common-right system did not preclude beneficial change, it certainly had a built-in bias against it. Potential individual enterprise was stifled by the need to reach communal decisions. Common rights to pasture gave rise to many long disputes. The system could scarcely cope with the problem of draining wet land.[3] The desperate shortage of fodder made it extremely difficult to overwinter livestocks; indeed, apart from sheep and cattle slaughtered before winter, the mortality rate during winter and early spring was high. There was a widespread tendency to exhaust the soil by overcropping. Traditional farming was characterized by a rigid separation of land into arable and pasture; crop-growing was treated as a separate branch of farming from stock-raising. Land productivity was capable of being greatly enhanced by combining these activities, and by shifting the use of land periodically between them. The shortage and inadequacy of implements meant a heavy demand for labour, especially at harvest times. Lack of capital, leadership and enterprise were also major handicaps to agricultural progress in many regions. Furthermore, in this context it should be emphasized that enclosure (i.e. the creation of compact farms) did not necessarily result in the adoption of superior techniques. Not all the enclosed areas were progressive, and some areas which had always been enclosed, for example the Weald of Kent and Sussex, were renowned for their backwardness.

Nevertheless, some progress could be seen, particularly in the ability of some landowners and farmers to respond to market forces. In the Tudor era, the area under pasture rose dramatically under the impact of an intense demand for wool. During the seventeenth century, and especially after the Restoration, a number of factors favoured a greater emphasis on grain and less on wool production. While some land still reverted from arable to pasture as wool production continued to increase, the rise in the area under grains reflected in some measure the cultivation of waste land. Agriculture also responded in the seventeenth century to a marked expansion in the demand for hides, meat, butter, cheese and milk. These intensified demands were associated in general with the rise in population and in particular with the growth of London and other industrial and commercial centres. And the satisfaction of these demands was made possible by rising productivity often as a result of regional specialization.

A spur to agricultural progress was the active land market. Under the Tudors the market was activated by the dissolution of the monasteries (in the 1530s) and the sale of Crown land to boost the revenue of hard-pressed monarchs. The even more hard-pressed early Stuart monarchs sold Crown land too. Again we should note that some landowners living beyond their means were forced to realize some of their holdings in order to liquidate debts. On the side of demand, some landowners were trying to enlarge and consolidate their estates, while sometimes wealthy merchants and professional men bought land as an investment and/or as a means of raising their social status. Of course, all land sales were not transfers from less to more progressive owners, but there can be no doubt that successful landowners were increasing their holdings and that some of the new blood was more commercially orientated than the old.

There is other evidence of progress. The late sixteenth and seventeenth centuries witnessed considerable building activity in the countryside. The expansion of agricultural output resulted in an increasing output of wool textiles, leather (boots, shoes, gloves, saddles), tallow (soap, candles), malt (beer, spirits), bones (glue), and so forth. From 1660, the output of grains was sufficiently great in many years to provide an exportable surplus. A considerable agricultural literature developed in the seventeenth century, and some experimentation took place. Indeed, the sixteenth and seventeenth centuries witnessed an agricultural revolution in the sense that new techniques and new crops became known. We shall consider the more important of these in the next chapter, but we shall contend that their adoption was slow, except perhaps in a few areas.

Industry

It is well known that Professor Nef has tried to convince his readers that Britain underwent an industrial revolution in the century beginning about 1540.[4] A number of industries were established in Britain over this period. If some of them were not new in the strictest sense, their output was negligible before the middle of the sixteenth century. Most of the industries were introduced from abroad, and were based on large-scale technology. The financial resources needed to take advantage of the production processes involved were far beyond the means of individual master-craftsmen. Nef emphasizes three important features of the changing economic scene. New enterprises were set up using, for that age, huge quantities of fixed-capital equipment. There was a large increase in the output and variety of manufactured products. And Britain was transformed from a predominantly wood-burning to a predominantly coal-burning economy.

In support of his thesis, Professor Nef draws attention to the building of paper-mills, saltpetre works and gunpowder mills, cannon foundries, sugar refineries, and copperas and alum factories. Copper was mined on a significant scale for the first time and, accompanying this development, brass-making and battery works were established. Blast furnaces were "vast structures", and the output of iron rose markedly down to 1610. The scale of manufacture in the sea-salt industry increased impressively, much larger quantities of sea water being evaporated. The output of salt might well have trebled between 1540 and 1640. Furnaces were built to make glass, the output of which rose to such an extent that, by the early seventeenth century, ordinary householders were installing glass windows. Soap-boiling and brewing also became significant industrial activities. The mining of lead increased greatly, and of coal spectacularly. According to one estimate, coal output advanced from somewhat more than 200,000 tons in 1550 to somewhat less than 3 million tons in 1700.

These developments had widespread implications for the British economy. The growth of the alum and copperas industries enabled dyers to obtain greater quantities of essential ingredients. Soap was required for scouring wool before it was made into cloth. Increasing supplies of salt enabled more fish, meat, butter and cheese to be preserved. The output of the metal trades expanded. Trade in coal gave a boost to the native ship-building industry. As the depth of mines increased so it became necessary to construct ventilation shafts, haulage devices, and drain water, usually by horse-power. The new large establishments employed "elaborate water-driven machinery". As the earlier industrial revolution got under way, the demand for timber rose sharply. For example, huge quantities of wood were consumed by the new blast furnaces. The growing scarcity and high price of timber stimulated the substitution of lead for wooden roofs, and a greater use of brick and stone and mortar in house-construction. But most important of all was the pressing need to substitute coal for wood in as many production processes as possible. If coal had not been readily available, the manufacturing sector of the British economy would have made far less progress than it did in the sixteenth and seventeenth centuries.

Coal, of course, was used by lime-burners and smiths in the Middle Ages.

However, in many industries, coal could not satisfactorily replace wood (or charcoal) until certain technical problems were overcome. In general, the problems were solved by erecting more complicated and expensive furnaces. Examples of industries in which coal became used are: salt, copperas and alum, saltpetre and gunpowder, soap, vinegar, pottery, brick, tile, glass, sugar-refining, starch – and candle-making, dyeing, brewing and distilling. Patents for baking bread with coal were taken out in 1635. And about the middle of the century, Derbyshire maltsters discovered a method of ridding coal of some impurities, thereby making coke which proved successful in drying malt. Nevertheless, large supplies of timber were still required in areas where lead, tin, copper and iron were smelted.

The Nef thesis may be criticized on two main grounds. While manufacturing industry certainly expanded between 1540 and 1640, while new techniques were introduced and developed, and while coal was substituted for wood as an industrial fuel to a significant extent, it does not follow that the British economy was thereby *transformed.* Industry in general was not suddenly characterized by large production units requiring heavy doses of fixed capital. These were exceptional, even probably in many of the industries cited by Professor Nef. Production units were typically small, and methods of production typically simple. It would be nearer the truth to say that in 1640 compared with 1540 industrial output consisted of more of the same. Apart from coal-mining, Professor Fisher sees "... little evidence of rapid industrial expansion before the second quarter of the seventeenth century".[5]

The advance of British manufacturing industry before about 1725 will be considered in later chapters. However, a few observations may be made at this juncture with special reference to the second reason for criticizing Professor Nef, namely that the decades after 1660 almost certainly witnessed more rapid economic development than the period which he reviewed. By way of a general comment on the extent of industrial activity in early eighteenth-century England, G.M. Trevelyan wrote: "To a bird's eye view England might have looked like a purely agricultural land, had not the bristling masts in every river-mouth told a tale of other activities than those of the peasant."[6] The increase and variety of manufactured exports after 1660 give a clear indication of considerable economic progress from that year. Towards the end of the seventeenth century, exports included many varieties of fully-finished textiles and of metal goods, pottery, glassware and leather goods. While cloth exports might have nearly doubled in value between 1660 and

and 1700, their relative importance declined because they accounted for about 75 per cent of total exports in the former year, but less than 50 per cent in the latter. Therefore, non-textile exports must have increased substantially over this period. Having cited these statistics, Professor Wilson tells us "... that it is doubtful whether even these increases in foreign trade reflect anything like the full extent of the industrial change and growth of those years. Indeed, preoccupation with exports may obscure and undervalue the growth of home markets."[7]

Apart from the increases in volume and value of domestically made products exported, there was a vast expansion in the import and re-export of colonial goods dating from the 1660s. Professor Davis has estimated that in 1699–1701 re-exports accounted for about 30 per cent of total exports.[8] The foundations of Britain's "Commercial Revolution" are well known. The Navigation Acts of 1651 and 1660, the Staple Act of 1663, the "dowry" brought by Catherine of Braganza on her marriage to Charles II, the Methuen Treaty of 1703, the defeat of Louis XIV's France in 1713, the Asiento Treaty of 1713, and the general commercial policy of successive governments all secured for British merchants by the early eighteenth century an unassailable position in the world carrying trade, and a considerable import-export trade.[9] The slave trade and the Newfoundland fishery were flourishing well before the end of the seventeenth century. By this time, hardly surprisingly, the ship-building industry was flourishing too, and was one of the largest employers of labour.[10] Warehouse-building, sugar-refining, and tobacco-processing were other industries to benefit from the growth of trade.

A number of developments created a more stable, encouraging, and competitive environment for industrial activity after 1660. The Restoration of Charles II came at the end of a twenty-year period of hostilities and uncertainty: the Civil Wars and the Interregnum were over. The exile of James II in the Glorious Revolution of 1688 marked the end of the conflict between the Stuart monarchs and Parliament and the beginning of greater religious toleration. The conclusion of the long European wars with the Treaty of Utrecht in 1713, the Hanoverian Succession on the death of Queen Anne in 1714, and the collapse of the Jacobite uprising in 1715 promised an era of peace at home and abroad. Post-Restoration governments were less paternalistic than those of Elizabeth I, James I and Charles I. Before the middle of the seventeenth century, governments tried to suppress inventions which threatened the livelihood of any group of workers. They also granted monopolies to the producers of many commodities including brass and copper, glass, paper, alum, saltpetre and soap. This practice hampered rather than stimulated industrial activity.[11] By contrast, the formation of companies to exploit inventions (i.e. to innovate) was encouraged by the Act of 1662 which limited the liability of shareholders. Especially after 1688, a large number of companies were floated, and their shares provided ample scope for the frenzied speculation which occurred after 1713 and culminated in the South Sea Bubble of 1720.[12] The attitude to the poor hardened; the Act of Settlement in 1662 gave parishes the power to evict any persons – unless they were born in the parish – who could or might not be able to support themselves. And the Act of 1723 ordered parishes to build workhouses, if necessary to unite to build them, and set the poor to work there. "Poverty was a form of original sin; the possession of wealth a form of salvation, the hall-mark of the elect."[13] We should also remember that the exclusion of dissenters from public office and the universities, which continued even though they were no longer persecuted after 1688, was an important factor in driving men imbued with the Protestant ethic into many business enterprises. After the Revocation of the Edict of Nantes in 1685, some 40,000 to 50,000 Huguenots migrated to Britain, and there were many skilled artisans among them. They made significant contributions to industries producing mathematical instruments, wool, linen and silk textiles, paper, glass, and other products.

The pace of innovation and the growth of industrial output were almost certainly faster after 1660 than before 1640. Hand-knitting, for example, spread rapidly throughout the country from the time of Henry VIII, when knitted nightcaps became all the rage. William Lee, a humble clergyman of Calverton, Nottinghamshire, invented a knitting-frame in 1589. The importance of this invention can hardly be exaggerated since it laid the foundation of the industry which would prove to be the first to use steam-power in factories. Yet there were few frames in use before the second half of the seventeenth century although, from the 1660s, the output of hosiery increased spectacularly. All branches of the textile industry benefited greatly from the use of new dyes, and new finishing methods in the decades before 1700. Innovative activity was probably stronger after than before 1660, partly because of the intensified demand for more attractive (colourful) and cheaper textiles at home and abroad, and partly because of the probable faster growth of output of agricultural products used in making dyes (e.g. weld – the dyer's weed, woad and madder). Again after 1660, the improved

"Saxony Wheel", giving a lighter thread, more rapidly superseded the distaff; and the introduction of the Dutch loom constituted an important technical advance in ribbon manufacture.[14] The first slitting-mills in the iron industry were established in the early seventeenth century; they slit iron into bars and rods which could then be put out to metal workers. But it was during the last four decades of the century that the output and variety of metal wares increased greatly. A strong demand emerged for these products; new skills were learned; and, before the turn of the century, the problem of smelting metallic ores (except iron) with coal had been solved. Both in terms of output and quality, our view is supported by reference to the pottery, paper and building industries. Professor Jones senses

> . . . a strong growth of domestic manufacturing in several industries (that) can definitely be assigned to the late seventeenth and early eighteenth centuries. It was important as a supplement to inadequate farm incomes, or in cases like Midland hosiery a remedy for the loss of agricultural work among those dispossessed by the enclosure of parishes which were laid down to pasture. . . . Domestic industries like cloth-making, hosiery, lace and leather work and nail-making thickened in the areas less favoured for farming. . . .[15]

The progress of manufacturing industry was also evidenced in endeavours after 1660 to make longer stretches of rivers navigable. The Act of Union (1707) made Britain a free trade area, and removed from Scotland all the disabilities imposed on her by the Navigation Acts. Finally, the rise in the number of patents granted, though obviously not an accurate indicator of technological progress, is worth noting: 31 (1660–69); 51 (1670–79); 53 (1680–89); and 102 (1690–99). Professor Wilson, after quoting these statistics, observes that the rate of innovation seen in the 1690s was not to reappear until after 1760.[16]

The Problem

In assessing the performance of the British economy during the second quarter of the eighteenth century, historians have advanced five views, only the first of which is fully consistent with any of the other four. Firstly, there is the long-standing consensus that the three or four decades ending about 1750 saw unprecedented prosperity for the great majority of the population. Certainly the thirties and forties were a golden age for the agricultural labourer. The harvests of these years (except 1739 and 1740) were so enormous that contemporaries could scarcely believe their eyes. " 'All history', one author declared, 'cannot furnish twenty such years of fertility and abundance as from 1730 to 1750 when the average prices were the lowest ever known.' "[17] Bread, the staple food, was so cheap that most labouring people must have sustained a notable rise in their standard of living. And we have often been reminded of the peace and prosperity of the country under the leadership of Robert Walpole, 1721 to 1742. J.L. and Barbara Hammond, of course, have stressed the fall in the purchasing power of wages as food prices advanced from the middle of the eighteenth into the nineteenth century.[18]

Many historians would agree with the theme of the last section, but would argue that the economic development of Britain during the decades after 1660 continued unabated throughout the eighteenth century and culminated in the Industrial Revolution. Admittedly there were fluctuations in activity and a few short-lived setbacks. Fluctuations were inevitable when the bulk of industrial output consisted of processed agricultural raw materials; and setbacks occurred as a result of harvest failures, abnormally high livestock mortality rates, wars, and financial and commodity speculations. But, according to this group of historians, and their view is probably the most widely held, the second quarter of the eighteenth century witnessed no discontinuity in Britain's economic advance. On the side of demand, the real income and therefore the real expenditure of most people were higher because of low food prices. On the side of supply, agricultural output was higher, much higher in the case of grains. Consequently there was more work on farms, more work distributing farm products, and more work in processing them. Industrial output was higher not only because of the greater supply of agricultural raw materials, but also in response to a more buoyant demand for non-food items. And merchants continued to prosper, benefiting from the trade-expansionary policies of Walpole. We shall examine this reasoning carefully in the following chapters.

The third view is that of Professor Nef, though probably with little following now. He believes that the upsurge in industrial activity which began in the sixteenth century was not maintained beyond the middle years of the seventeenth century. He sees the whole period from the mid-seventeenth to the mid-eighteenth century as one of slackening economic development, more or less an interlude between the earlier industrial revolution and the renewed vigorous expansion dating from the 1750s and leading into the factory age. Thus he writes of " ... the slowing down of progress towards industrialism in England [between 1660 and 1750] ".[19] We have already given some reasons why we cannot accept this verdict, and additional arguments will be offered later. Nevertheless, it is true that economic advance could have been more rapid than it was after 1660. The persecution of dissenters from the early 1660s to 1688 must have had some stifling effect on enterprise. Abraham Darby I used coke to smelt iron for the first time in 1709, but, as we noted earlier, maltsters were using coke at least half a century before that date: why the delay when charcoal was so expensive, and iron a key raw material? Some kind of steam engine might have been invented by the Marquis of Worcester in the mid-seventeenth century, yet the major break-through in steam-power technology came much later in 1708 when Newcomen took out a patent for his engine. Again we ask why the delay when the difficulty of draining mines was so acute? Finally we note, though without conviction, another argument of Professor Nef to illustrate his case for retarded economic growth over 1660 to 1750, namely, ". . . the renewal of an older civilized emphasis on artistic workmanship [in the pottery industry] ".[20]

Dr. Clarkson has recently provided us with a fourth view, and it must rate the most pessimistic. For him, the second quarter of the eighteenth century came at the end of two centuries or more of stagnation. Clearly a stagnating economy has hardly the strength to decelerate! In his opinion, the whole period from 1500 to 1750 was characterized by a "painfully slow" increase in *per capita* real income; little technical advance in most industries, transport and commerce; and a generally unskilled labour force. Production was labour-intensive, and labour productivity was low. In so far as technical progress occurred, it tended to be a feature of less important industries such as mining and metallurgy. Given almost universal poverty and economic backwardness, the incentive to change production functions and develop markets was low. Whatever exceptions and qualifications ought to be made, ". . . the fact remains that English economic history before 1750 is in a large measure the story of economic stagnation".[21] Such a gloomy picture inevitably emerges if one compares progress in pre-industrial England with the pace of advance during and after her industrialization in the nineteenth and twentieth centuries.

Finally, limited support has been forthcoming in recent years for the hypothesis that a large part of the second quarter of the eighteenth century witnessed a discontinuity in the pace of growth, a slowing down in the rate of development, and possibly a retreat in one or two sectors of the British economy. The *locus classicus* of the case for deceleration between about 1725 and 1750 is the regional study of Professor Chambers, "*Vale of Trent, 1670–1800*".[22] Although this survey is confined to the north-east Midlands area, it should be remembered that this region witnessed the break-through in textile technology. Moreover, Chambers believed his conclusions had a much wider geographic applicability, and he had no doubt that the economic progress in many sectors of the economy during the late seventeenth and early eighteenth centuries petered out around the year 1730, if not before, and the next two decades saw comparative stagnation. We are inclined to the view that, in some industries, deceleration might have set in even before 1720. Strong support for the Chambers hypothesis has come from Deane and Cole who state unequivocally that nearly all production indices show the economy was stagnating during the two decades ending about 1745. Professor Wilson sees a long pause ". . . from the 1720s to the 1740s, when all the forces of growth seemed to be weak".[23] Taken together, the work of many economic historians provides a formidable case for supposing that the development of the British economy faltered between the late twenties and the late forties. Our purpose is to bring together, review, and strengthen that case.

Notes

1 F.J. Fisher, "The Sixteenth and Seventeenth Centuries: The Dark Ages in English Economic History?", *Economica*, 1957, p.15; J.D. Chambers, *Nottinghamshire in the Eighteenth Century*, second edition, 1966, pp.xiii–xiv.

2 Eric Kerridge, *The Agricultural Revolution*, 1967, p.326; H.C. Pawson, *Robert Bakewell*, 1957, p.4.

3 "Even if his (a farmer's) neighbours were willing to let him connect a surface ditch with one they had made themselves, there was little hope of the same indulgence for hollow, or underground drainage. The inability of the system to deal with the problem of wet lands was perhaps the chief of its drawbacks." (T.S. Ashton, *An Economic History of England: The Eighteenth Century*, 1955, p.34.)

4 J.U. Nef, "The Progress of Technology and Growth of Large-Scale Industry in Great Britain, 1540–1640", *Economic History Review*, 1934; and, *The Rise of the British Coal Industry*, 1932, second impression 1966, vol. 1, part II, chapters II and III.

5 F.J. Fisher, op.cit., p.16. See also L.A. Clarkson, *The Pre-Industrial Economy in England, 1500–1750*, 1971, pp.115-16.

6 G.M. Trevelyan, *England under Queen Anne* 1930, vol. 1, p.6.

7 C.H. Wilson, *England's Apprenticeship, 1603–1763*, 1965, p.185.
8 Ralph Davis, "English Foreign Trade, 1660–1700", *Economic History Review*, 1954, p.150.
9 The Navigation Acts and the Staple Act gave a virtual monopoly of British and Empire trade to British and Empire shipping. Christopher Hill says that "Charles II's marriage to Catherine of Braganza has been described as virtually a condition of his restoration. . . . With Catherine came Bombay, direct trade (slaves) with Portuguese West Africa and with Brazil (sugar, partly for re-export, and gold). With her also came Tangier, England's first base in the Mediterranean. . ." (*Reformation to Industrial Revolution*, 1968, p.129). The Methuen Treaty gave Portugal a preferential tariff on her wines, and in exchange her market was opened for British textiles. The Asiento Treaty broke Spain's monopoly of the South American slave trade.
10 Ralph Davis, "Merchant Shipping in the Economy of the Late Seventeenth Century", *Economic History Review*, 1956, p.59; and *The Rise of the English Shipping Industry in the Seventeenth and Eighteenth Centuries*, 1962, chapter II; D.C. Coleman, "Naval Dockyards under the Later Stuarts", *Economic History Review*, 1953.
11 L.A. Clarkson, *The Pre-Industrial Economy in England 1500–1750*, 1971, pp.112, 160-1, 174.
12 Lord Macaulay, *History of England* (Firth's edition), 1914, vol. V, chapter XIX, pp.2,275-80; W.R. Scott, *The Constitution and Finance of English, Scottish and Irish Joint Stock Companies to 1720*, 1911, vol. II, pp.438-9.
13 J.D. Chambers, op.cit., p.48.
14 L.A. Clarkson, op.cit., pp.106, 112; C.H. Wilson, op.cit., p.185.
15 E.L. Jones (ed.), "Agricultural Productivity and Economic Growth, 1700–1760", in *Agriculture and Economic Growth in England, 1650–1815*, 1967, p.37.
16 C.H. Wilson, op.cit., pp.187-8.
17 Cited by G.E. Mingay, "The Agricultural Depression, 1730–1750", *Economic History Review*, 1956, p.336.
18 J.L. and B. Hammond, *The Village Labourer*, fourth edition, 1926, p.87.
19 J.U. Nef, *War and Human Progress*, 1950, p.175.
20 ibid.
21 L.A. Clarkson, op.cit., especially pp.10, 13, 16-17, 22, 106.
22 J.D. Chambers, "Vale of Trent, 1670–1800", *Economic History Review*, 1957, Supplement no. 3. His general conclusions appear on p.3.
23 Phyllis Deane and W.A. Cole, *British Economic Growth, 1688–1959*, second edition 1967, pp.61, 91-2; C.H. Wilson, op.cit., p.359.

2 AGRICULTURE

> There is, however, an important difference between our lot and that of our forebears. Most of them earned their bread on the soil. . . . The prodigality or niggardliness of the landlord mattered less than the prodigality or niggardliness of nature; what was happening at Westminster or in the City was of small account compared with what was happening in the heavens. (T.S. Ashton)

> It can be deduced from Gregory King's estimates (1688) that

> . . . *primarily* agricultural families . . . account for about 68 per cent of the total (population). By 1750 the proportion had almost certainly fallen somewhat . . . but it probably still lay between about 60 and 70 per cent. (Phyllis Deane)[1]

The Course of Agricultural Prices

The prices of farm products were significant for a number of reasons. In the first place, the landed gentry and the larger tenant farmers benefited when prices were high, but their incomes were depressed when prices were low. We should bear in mind here that the landed interest was a major source of financial capital in Britain during the seventeenth and eighteenth centuries. Secondly, the incomes of farmers varied partly with the quantities of their marketable surpluses (i.e. their output less their own requirements), and partly with ruling prices for their produce. Thus many farmers were adversely affected by either the combination of high prices and low output or the combination of low prices and high output. Thirdly, as many wage rates were fairly constant until about 1770/80, the purchasing power of most labourers and other groups changed inversely with the trend of agricultural prices. These prices, of course, figured far more prominently than today in the "cost of living". And finally, the prices of some farm products were cost prices of some industrial raw materials.

We recognize at the outset that the interpretation of price data involves difficulties. If the prices of some farm products moved in a different direction from others, how can we identify an overall trend? Even if nearly all prices were rising or falling together, the comparative rates of change might differ considerably, so how can we measure an overall rate of change? The time series for a few agricultural prices might give distorted or false impressions of general price movements of farm products with regard to both their direction and magnitude. Owing to poor communications, at least before the late eighteenth century, the country consisted of a number of regional economies, and hence the price of the same product might have differed from centre to centre. For example, comparative prices for wheat sold at Exeter, Eton and Winchester reveal that disparities could at times be very marked.[2] To raise these problems amounts to a demand for an accuracy which is impossible owing to lack of data and for statistical reasons of a technical nature.

There is no need for preoccupation with the difficulties touched on in the last paragraph. Agriculture in many regions during the seventeenth and eighteenth centuries was characterized by a pronounced tendency towards raising a variety of crops and livestock. Patterns of production usually allowed some (though limited) flexibility. Decisions of producers must have been influenced to some extent by changes in the relative profitability of different products occasioned by changes in their relative prices. In addition, consumers must have changed the pattern of their spending in response to changes in relative agricultural prices. We can safely assume therefore that the switching of effort towards relatively dearer products by producers, and the switching of expenditure towards relatively cheaper products by consumers would have tended, given time, to moderate different comparative rates of change of prices. Apart from these substitution effects, we should recall the extent of inter-regional trade which reduced price disparities for the same product. Despite the bad roads, a large volume of traffic in farm products was facilitated by navigable waterways and by the ability of livestock to transport themselves.[3] Furthermore, it should be remembered that seasonal conditions, especially frosts and droughts, were usually pervasive in their effect upon the output and hence the price of a product or a range of products. Finally, we believe our thesis can be supported without detailed agricultural price data.

Much of the statistical information on which we base the following description of the course of agricultural prices is derived from Sir William Beveridge's *Prices and Wages in England* (1939).[4] The prices of grains were high in the 1660s, in the so-called "barren years" from 1692–9, and rather high generally between 1708 and 1715, and between 1727 and 1729. But the secular trend was unmistakably downwards. Low prices prevailed over 1675 to 1691, especially the years 1686–91, and again in most years between 1700 and 1730, very low levels being reached over the next two decades (except 1739–40). The markets for wheat, barley and oats reached their nadir in 1743, 1745 and 1747 respectively. Wheat prices, for instance, in the southern part of England and perhaps elsewhere, ruled 25 to 33 per cent lower in the 1730s and 1740s than their average level of the 1660s.

It is difficult to find a definite trend of meat prices during the period before the mid-eighteenth century. They seemed to reach a peak around 1658–64 after which, apart from fluctuations and the occasional year of great abundance or scarcity, they were fairly stable until the 1730s. London prices changed little from the late 1660s to 1730, although mutton prices at Eton were rather lower over 1700–30 than over 1670–1700. London and Eton prices slumped to low levels in the 1730s and 1740s, especially between 1734 and 1748, and more markedly for mutton than for beef.

There is no reason to suppose that most other farm products had a price history very different from that of grains and meat. Wool prices were on a downward trend from the early 1660s, very low prices being recorded over the years 1734–42, the latter year seeing the prices of both wool and tallow at their lowest. The wool clip might well have increased by about one half between the last decade of the seventeenth century and the early 1740s, but its total value could have fallen, reflecting a dramatic fall in prices over this period.[5] Dairy farmers fared better than most other producers because the prices of milk, butter and cheese were fairly stable from the mid-1660s. However, even these prices receded, particularly in London, during the 1730s.

Agricultural prices turned the corner in the 1740s, but no speedy advance took place. Grain prices were somewhat higher from the late forties to the early sixties, after which they moved forward sharply. In the case of wheat, increases were on the order of 15 to 20 per cent (1745/55 – 1755/65), but prices more than doubled between the middle and the end of the century. The prices of meat ruled at somewhat higher levels in the late forties and fifties, but it was not until the mid-sixties that markets began to surge ahead. Between 1743 and 1780, wool prices fluctuated about a level some 20–25 per cent above that of 1735–42, but they were carried (along with most prices) to higher levels in the last two decades of the century. And the prices of dairy products gained ground from the early forties, and fluctuated about a rising trend for the remainder of the century.

Certain aspects of these price movements are particularly important from our viewpoint. Markets for most agricultural products weakened from the 1660s, and the downward trend, though not continuous, stretched over the very long period ending in the 1740s. There were many years when prices, especially those of grains, were either very high or very low. By and large, prices were very low indeed in the 1730s and 1740s, most low points being reached in the last decade. Although the late forties and fifties saw prices at rather higher levels, recovery did not firmly set in until the sixties.

The Earlier Agricultural Revolution

Despite a gently rising population and grain exports which were particularly heavy during the thirties and forties, the increasing supply of agricultural products could be absorbed only on a secularly declining price level. This trend appears to support the now widely held view that British agriculture *in general* was vigorously progressive between the late sixteenth (certainly between the mid-seventeenth) and the mid-eighteenth century. As will be seen in the next section, this is a view we do not share. For example, we shall stress the limited extent to which innovations took place before 1750–60. Nevertheless, there can be no doubt that, between about 1550 and 1750, the productive *potential* of British agriculture increased beyond measure. In this respect, we agree with Dr. Kerridge that an agricultural revolution took place.[6]

"The backbone of the agricultural revolution was the conversion of permanent tillage and permanent grassland or of temporary and shifting cultivations, to permanently cultivated arable alternating between temporary tillage and temporary grass leys. The new husbandry . . . is nowadays called 'ley farming', convertible, alternate or 'field-grass' husbandry."[7] Both permanent pasture and common fields were made over to convertible husbandry after 1560, and especially between 1590 and 1660. Dr. Kerridge estimates that such transfers would have resulted in a doubling of output and a reduction in costs, total unit costs being less than one-quarter of those incurred in common-field husbandry. A temporary grass ley supported twice the stock of permanent pasture, and four times the stock of common fields. It follows that the adoption of the new husbandry would have brought about a much larger output of industrial by-products such as wool and hides. Wool production, for example, might have been increased eightfold. In general, the move from permanent arable and permanent pasture to convertible husbandry resulted in a doubling of grain yields.[8]

Many new crops were grown before 1650, and they were incorporated into new rotations well before the end of the seventeenth century. Both common-field and convertible husbandry were modified in order to take advantage of the new practices. The most important innovations were the cultivation of root crops (turnips, carrots, parsnips, swedes) and artificial – i.e. deliberately sown – grasses (clovers, sainfoin, trefoil, rye-grass, lucerne). Of these, turnips and clover have received most attention from historians but the significance of other crops should not be underestimated. Together they gave many farmers the opportunity of massively increasing their output. Unproductive fallows were either less necessary or unnecessary. A field of clover yielded three times or more fodder than one of natural grass. Turnips were used as fodder not only to overwinter livestock but to fatten them for the market. By feeding tops and roots to livestock, farmers obtained a richer manure which was very useful for consolidating light, sandy soils. The artificial grasses caused the soil to be fertilized through a process of nitrogen-fixation and, indirectly, they provided richer manure. In short, the age-old winter fodder shortage could be eliminated, and so the country could support a far greater livestock population. Soil fertility could be much improved through more and richer manure and through nitrogen-fixation so that grain and other yields could be much enhanced.

The technique of floating water-meadows began to spread from the late sixteenth century, and this development promised further gains in the same directions. Briefly, the floated water-meadow was a device by which farmers could irrigate land bordering on or lying close to a stream or river. Water was forced through a weir or hatch, channelled through trenches or ducts, and so induced to flow over the meadow. The flow of water protected grass from frost and encouraged its early growth. Not only could more livestock be overwintered with the prospect of early grass, but the grass and hay of the water-meadows were excellent feed, and the quantity could have been four or more times as great as before irrigation. Dr. Kerridge tells us that: "Arable was converted to rich meadow, raising its annual value six, eight or tenfold."[9]

A number of seventeenth-century writers stressed the importance of the new agriculture. Walter Blith emphasized the need to drain heavy (clay) soils, the desirability of floating water-meadows, and the advantages to be gained by periodically converting arable to pasture and *vice versa.* He also advocated the growing of turnips and the generous use of manure and fertilizers: the application of lime, for example, had in some areas made formerly barren land capable of raising grains. Among other writers, John Worlidge strongly advised the floating of water-meadows, and Sir Richard Weston the growing of artificial grasses such as clover and sainfoin.[10] We conclude that few historians would dispute the verdict of Mr. Trow-Smith: "The seventeenth century had largely set the seal of perfection upon agricultural practice as it knew it. Its ways have persisted in very many details down to our own day . . ."[11]

Agricultural Deceleration and Stagnation

Having outlined the more important features of the earlier agricultural revolution, we must now consider the likely rate at which the new techniques were adopted. By the year 1700, the new artificial grasses (especially clover) and the new roots (especially turnips) were grown in a number of counties. A variety of crops were being introduced and incorporated into new rotations. The technique of the floated water-meadow gained acceptance in parts of southern England before 1700, and in parts of the eastern and midland counties afterwards. Convertible husbandry became increasingly adopted, even in some open-field villages. Land was enclosed and laid down for pasture, and sheep population increased markedly after 1660 in some midland counties, particularly Leicestershire. Soil fertility was raised by the use of chalk, lime and marl. In short, many historians over the last twenty years or more have multiplied time and time again examples of agricultural progress between 1600 and 1750, and with such enthusiasm that it is difficult to resist the conclusion that the majority of English farmers (outside the clay soil zones with their drainage problem) had adopted the new techniques wherever applicable.[12] Furthermore, it has been suggested that the downward trend of agricultural prices not only reflected in large measure the diffusion of the new techniques but, especially in the 1730s and 1740s, accelerated this diffusion or at least strengthened the inducement to use more efficient methods to raise output in order to cushion the impact of very low prices on farmers' profits and landowners' rents.[13]

We believe that, taking the country as a whole, the new agriculture was making slow headway before 1750 or 1760, and that low profitability impeded rather than stimulated the development of the farm sector. It is possible that additions to the area under cultivation were collectively as important as innovations in accounting for larger agricultural output. For instance, the period 1550 to 1750 witnessed considerable deforestation and enclosure of wastes. In so far as technical advances were achieved, we need to consider the likely scale of innovational activity. Paradoxically at first sight the remarkable productivity of the new grasses, roots and water-meadows is itself one reason for doubting whether they were in extensive use before the late eighteenth century. Against the enormous increases in productive potential (some of which we mentioned in the last section) has to be set the limited capacity of markets to absorb much greater farm surpluses, at least before the 1760s. Given the slow rise in population and the very gradual improvement at most in communications, only the sluggish diffusion of the new techniques is consistent with the failure of agricultural prices to fall dramatically before the second quarter of the eighteenth century. Their decline during the thirties and forties is probably explained less by the rate of innovation than by the following factors: the check to population growth over much of this period; the bumper harvests due mainly to the weather; the rise in sheep population associated in part with the conversion of some arable to pasture under pressure to reduce labour costs, and in part with the desire to take advantage of the larger numbers of cattle from Scotland bound for the pastures of East Anglia for fattening before being driven to the London abattoirs; and the increasing pig population which was largely a by-product of the expanding distillery industry. It is interesting to note also that the export demand for grains, even from areas most accessible to Europe, was insufficiently elastic to prevent sharp falls in prices.[14]

This reasoning would be seriously weakened had British farmers been faced with expanding and buoyant markets overseas. There is no foundation for such an assumption. Agricultural prices were on a downward trend in Western Europe as well as in Britain from the mid-seventeenth to the mid-eighteenth century.[15] For British agriculture, export demand was significant only for wool (in the form of textiles) and for grains. As we have seen, the prices of these products were declining for much of the period from the 1660s to the 1740s. Half (or even more than half) the output of wool textiles was exported but, since foreign governments usually raised trade barriers to protect their own textile industries, the capacity of potential markets for British exporters was clearly limited. No wonder John Methuen's Treaty of 1703 which diverted Portuguese textile trade in Britain's favour was hailed as a commercial *coup.* The battle for outlets abroad had already been indicated by the Act of 1699 which placed an embargo on all Irish exports of wool or wool textiles to all foreign and colonial markets. And the long-standing export duty on wool textiles had been cancelled in 1700. Furthermore, the export of wool textiles might well have been increasing at a slower rate than that of output.[16] Turning to grains, we note that many historians have stressed the large volume of exports between 1660 and 1760, so large perhaps as to justify the description of Britain as "the Granary of Europe". Statistics do not bear out this claim for only rarely was more than 5 per cent of total production shipped abroad.[17]

Dr. Kerridge has estimated that the output of foodstuffs at least doubled between 1540 and 1700, and that it at least kept pace with population growth.[18] This record is far from impressive given the greater area of land under crops or enclosed for pasture, and given the far higher yields of which much land was capable. There is good evidence for the snail's pace at which new knowledge was disseminated and acted upon before the second half of the eighteenth century. The field cultivation of turnips was a firmly established practice in Norfolk and Suffolk by the 1660s, yet it is well known that Townshend, who did not devote himself to his Norfolk estate until 1730, eventually earned himself an immense reputation by incorporating turnips in his crop rotations and popularizing the idea. But his attempts to persuade other landowners and farmers to follow his example were far from successful for many years. Professor Mathias believes that Townshend's influence on other landowners came only after a considerable time-lag: ". . . increasingly the aristocracy followed his lead *after 1750*". And this view is shared by Professor Heaton who writes: "The new husbandry spread slowly at first. Townshend's farmers were loath to spend time, labour, and money on drilling seed or hoeing turnips. . ."[19] Similarly Coke, who inherited his Norfolk estate in 1776, became renowned for recommending farm practices some of which had been used by his ancestors half a century and more previously.[20]

Many historians have commented on the fact that Tull's seed-drill and horse-hoe, invented about 1701 and 1714 respectively, met with indifference and hostility, even after he published his *Horse-Hoeing Husbandry* in 1733. Writing in 1770, Arthur Young noted "The new husbandry" as having sunk with Tull, and "not again put in motion till within a few years".[21] Young emphasized that many farmers used wastefully heavy teams and cumbersome ploughs, when lighter ploughs and smaller teams would have accomplished the same work more cheaply. He came across many areas where the new fodder crops were little known or little used. Young of course did not begin his publishing career until the late sixties and, even when allowance is made for his tendency to exaggerate, the fact remains that his works indicate the extent to which the new methods had been neglected. For Naomi Riches, Young "... did more than any other one person to popularize Norfolk husbandry", while Coke was "the real hero of Norfolk agriculture".[22]

Other examples of the slow adoption of improved agricultural practices can be cited. In 1663, the well-known writer Andrew Yarranton, published his *Improvement by Clover*, yet Lord Ernle is convinced that "... in 1768 clover was still unknown in many counties".[23] Professor Hamilton reports that turnips were first grown near Melrose in 1747, "causing great consternation among the people". He describes Ayrshire as "very progressive" but, "... when Wight visited the county in 1773, the new methods of agriculture were only beginning to be adopted by the mass of the people".[24] Henry Rowlands, an Anglesea vicar from 1696 to 1723, wrote up many experiments in his *Idea Agriculturae,* but "... a full generation after his death, when his essay was still unpublished, a traveller described the island as 'a naked and unpleasant country... uncultivated still... so that I am told it does not produce a tenth of what the land is capable of' ".[25] The limited scale on which the new practices had been adopted is clearly indicated by the spate of agricultural literature, societies, shows and competitions dating from the 1760s, and later the establishment of the Board of Agriculture in 1793, all of which amounted to a vast and unremitting campaign to popularize the new agriculture. However, except for improvements in stock-breeding, most of the "new" techniques had been known for many decades, some for over a century.

We cannot say precisely when agricultural deceleration began, but our best guess would be during the last decade of the seventeenth century and certainly no later than the early eighteenth century. The 1730s and 1740s witnessed stagnation and depression, at least in some regions. The downturn of agricultural prices from the 1660s suggests that the increase in output quickened between then and the period of very poor harvests over 1692–9. The subsequent desperately low rate of innovation is strongly implied by Deane and Cole's estimate that, based on an index with 1700 = 100, real agricultural output increased to 111 in 1750, to 117 in 1770, and then rose to 143 in 1800.[26] We shall contend that the profitability of farming and the expected rate of return on agricultural investment dominated the pace of agricultural advance both before and after the year 1700. The earlier agricultural revolution (1540–1700) was characterized by an accumulation of new knowledge and a widespread failure to apply it.[27] By contrast, the outstanding feature of the agricultural revolution (1750–1880) was the enormous increase in the output of nearly all farm products. The earlier agricultural revolution ran out of steam not because, as Dr. Kerridge asserts, the spread of innovations was almost completed, but because even the limited adoption of new techniques together with the cultivation of previously barren, waste, or common land reduced the profitability of farming.[28] Agricultural progress was retarded not only by the problems of diffusing new ideas but by other factors such as the small farmers' lack of capital, the survival of open fields and communal husbandry, and the need for revision of tenures and renewal of farm buildings. It must be stressed that one advance could often have been achieved only if accompanied by associated advances, and hence the cost of improvement might have been considerable.

The increase in output from 1660 (we must emphasize again) was accompanied by falling prices; the increase in output from 1760 by rising prices. Rents and estate incomes rose substantially from 1640 to 1690, and again from the mid-1760s into the first decade of the nineteenth century. On the whole, rents were fairly steady from 1690 to 1720 or 1730; they were under pressure during the next twenty years, after which they began to recover. Between 1690 and 1750, rents rarely increased by more than 40 per cent and a figure of less than 15 per cent was far more common. Over the same period, except where landowners enlarged or improved their estates, their income (net of land tax, administrative expenses, and concessions to impoverished tenants) barely increased at all.[29] The period 1690 to 1730 was characterized by wide variations in output, reflecting harvest fluctuations and sometimes the incidence of animal disease. Since many farms were small, profits suffered either because an unduly large output was confronted by a relatively inelastic demand or because an unduly small output permitted only a small or no marketable surplus.[30] Even specialist grain farmers found their profits curbed to some extent in time of famine owing to measures to ban exports and to control the price of bread. The 1730s and 1740s were a critical period not only because the prices of farm products fell to their lowest levels of the century, but because these years followed four decades when conditions, more often than not, were unfavourable to farmers and landowners.

This summary of the trend of rents, net estate incomes and profits inevitably masks the experience of some landowners and farmers. Thus some rents were reduced between 1690 and 1720, while some moved against the subsequent downward trend.[31] The profits of dairy farmers might have held up, except perhaps in the worst years of the thirties. But there seems to be a consensus that conditions were adverse (or at least not favourable) for the farm sector in many years from the early 1690s and that, especially in the thirties and forties, profits were squeezed between low prices on the one hand and relatively sticky production costs on the other.

We must now examine the case for believing that the difficulties of landowners and farmers down to the mid-eighteenth century stimulated agricultural progress. There was clearly pressure to reduce costs either by substituting products which required less labour (for example, wool for grains) or by using more efficient techniques, or both (for example, new crop rotations). Investment was encouraged as a means of raising output and of substituting more for less profitable land use. Landowners sought competent stewards to improve the administration of their estates, and good tenants found themselves in demand. The shift in the balance of bargaining power between tenants and landowners induced the latter to spend more on estate maintenance and capital items. They repaired buildings and fences, and erected new ones. They had roads repaired and hedges planted. They paid for the clearing and fertilizing of land, and even gave seed to their tenants. These activities of some landowners, which were certainly in evidence during the thirties and forties, were the outcome of three main factors. In the first place, very low agricultural prices placed a financial burden on tenants which was either very difficult or impossible for them to shoulder without assistance. Secondly, a new breed of landowners appeared during the period 1680 to 1720. Professor Habakkuk advises us that ". . . the new purchasers were not seeking good speculations, but well-tenanted estates which would yield a regular income with a minimum of trouble".[32] The third factor was the cheapness and availability of mortgages.[33]

This account of agricultural progress through adversity is one-sided and we believe there are more convincing reasons for the view that, on balance, the development of the agricultural sector was hampered by low profitability and low prices before 1750. Admittedly in some areas such as East Anglia with its light, sandy soil, farmers and landowners cushioned to some extent the effect of low prices by raising output, and it is just possible that some of them suffered little or no fall in income.[34] Perhaps it should be stressed here that north-west Norfolk was a highly exceptional area, with unusually large farms let at very low rents to tenants who were expected to invest heavily in marl and manures. By contrast, in areas with mainly clay soils (e.g. the Midlands) with their drainage problem, the new practices were less applicable and hence usually output could not be significantly increased. The success of some farmers and landowners in reducing the impact of low prices on their incomes had some counterpart in lowering the incomes of others. The adoption of new techniques in some regions (thereby causing output to rise further and prices to fall further) were partly responsible for an intensified squeeze on profits or widespread losses in non-innovating regions. Professor Mingay's research on the records of the Duke of Kingston's estates in Nottinghamshire revealed ". . . numerous changes of tenants, alterations of holdings and divisions of farms, rent abatements, reports of tenants 'throwing up', and distraints upon their effects". Some landowners paid the land tax during the depression, but shifted it back to the tenantry in the fifties and sixties.[35] In the face of this evidence, we cannot exclude the possibility that some land fell out of cultivation during the thirties and forties. The flexibility of farming, of course, was limited by the survival of open fields, and by bad transport conditions. In many cases, the introduction of one improvement was dependent on introducing others: rotations could not be changed on heavy soils unless effective drainage was provided; conversion to grass involved heavy expenditure on seed, and required capital, and so on. Hard-pressed farmers were often reluctant to buy manure, fertilizer and seed, even though such purchases might have been well worth-while. Indeed, this was one of the reasons for Young's attacks on small-scale farming, and his belief that agricultural progress depended on large-scale farming. Furthermore, in areas where the aim of estate management was to minimize losses or where profits had been driven to very low levels, innovational activity was probably discouraged. Here we have in mind not only the psychological argument that the risk of experimentation or change of farming practice would have loomed larger, but the economic argument that the costs of many of the new methods were high. They were usually labour-intensive, making for higher labour costs per acre and perhaps sometimes per unit of output.[36]

Of even greater significance than the high variable costs of the new agriculture were the heavy fixed costs (associated with enclosure and building) which often had to be incurred before common land could be brought into cultivation and more efficient methods of farming adopted. Professor Fisher did not mince words when he wrote: "The main form of agricultural improvement was the enclosure of open fields and commons – it is estimated that two acres of enclosed land were worth three in the open fields or seven on the commons. . ."[37] We do not deny that there were improvements in the period before 1750, but they were aimed chiefly at helping farmers survive in difficult times; expansion of output was a secondary consideration until prices rose after 1750/60.. Much investment during the second quarter of the eighteenth century was forced on landowners in order to keep their holdings financially viable. It was replacement rather than net investment, short- rather than long- term investment, and hence with little or no long-term implications for agricultural development. It was investment motivated by the instinct for survival rather than the desire to maximize long-run profits and rents. There was a lull in building activity in the countryside between about 1725 and 1760.[38] The number of enclosure acts averaged about four a year between 1700 and 1760, but from then until 1792 the figure leapt to over forty a year. According to one estimate, nearly half a million acres were enclosed by parliamentary acts between 1761 and 1792, compared with less than 75,000 acres between 1727 and 1760.[39] Professor Ashton has noted that ". . . the only years that show distinct activity in Parliament (during the first half of the eighteenth century) are 1729–30 and 1742–43 – both periods following deficient harvests and relatively high prices of food".[40] The causal relationship between higher prices of farm products, higher incomes of landowners, and the rate of enclosure during the late eighteenth century is not disputed, but it suggests that agricultural progress before 1750 was retarded by low prices, profits and rents. We do not pretend to understand the view that British agriculture was vigorously progressive under the influence of both the stick (before 1750) and the carrot (afterwards).

Professor Habakkuk has drawn attention to the growth of estates in the late seventeenth and early eighteenth centuries, and the more rational approach of the new landowners who saw their estates not only as a symbol of their stature, but also as business concerns.[41] For most of the wealthier landowners it cannot be said that they could not afford outlays on enclosure. Unlike the gentry of the seventeenth century, they often had two or three incomes – from land, public office, army or navy commissions, and/or mining. Their expenditure was prodigal in all directions except that of productive investment. They spent vast sums on their homes, ransacked Europe to adorn them, sent their sons on the Grand Tour – the aristocratic tourist industry, as Professor Wilson reminds us, was flourishing by the mid-eighteenth century.[42] Their hospitality was incredible, guests staying weeks, months, even years. If they could incur prodigious debts in financing such lavish and ostentatious expenditure, why could they not raise finance or why were they unwilling to raise finance for long-term investment in agriculture? We believe that the long period of relatively low agricultural profitability with the worst years between 1730 and 1750 must have seriously reduced the incentive to undertake enclosure and long-term improvement. Indeed, the expected rate of return on long-term investment in agriculture might at times have been negative. It was not falling interest rates from the 1720s but the rising profitability of farming from the 1760s that set off an enclosure movement which transformed the English countryside.

Finally, the history of land reclamation, especially attempts to drain the fens, that huge waterlogged area of eastern England bordering on the Wash, lends support to the deceleration--stagnation thesis as applied to agriculture. Considerable drainage activity took place between 1560 and 1660, and Charles I in particular showed much interest in both the planning and execution of work in the 1630s. Less intensified effort marked the long period from 1660 to 1720, the main reason being that lower grain prices reduced the incentive to sink capital into land reclamation. Serious floodings occurred in the early 1660s, 1673, 1687 and 1693, and these were in some measure the result of failure to carry out adequate repairs. But worse was to come. In Dr. Kerridge's words, ". . . between 1720 and 1735, during the lowest depths of depression, fen drainage was allowed to go to rack and ruin." It was not until the second half of the eighteenth century that renewed efforts were made to recover flooded land. But by this time land was becoming more and more valuable as the profitability of agriculture improved. To quote Professor Mathias: "Drainage acts were equivalent in the fens to enclosure acts elsewhere and had similar results."[43]

Notes

1 T.S. Ashton, *Economic Fluctuations in England, 1700–1800*, 1959, p.2; Phyllis Deane, *The First Industrial Revolution*, 1967, pp.13-14, her italics.

2 See the Table of B.R. Mitchell and Phyllis Deane, *Abstract of British Historical Statistics*, 1962, pp.486-7.

3 The impressive scale of internal commerce can be judged by reference to Defoe's *Tour through England and Wales* (first published 1724–7) and R.B. Westerfield's *Middlemen in English Business, particularly between 1660 and 1760*, 1915.

4 Other sources are: Tooke and Newmarch, *A History of Prices*, 1838, reprinted 1928, especially pp.38-51; A.H. John, "The Course of Agricultural Change, 1660–1760", in L.S. Pressnell (ed.), *Studies in the Industrial Revolution*,

presented to T.S. Ashton, 1960; A.H. John, "Agricultural Productivity and Economic Growth, 1700–1760", *Journal of Economic History*, 1965, and reprinted in E.L. Jones (ed.), *Agriculture and Economic Growth*, 1967; T.S. Ashton, *Economic Fluctuations in England, 1700–1800*, 1959, chapter 1.

5 This statement is implied by the estimates of Miss Deane. See Table 3 below, chapter 4, p.64.

6 Eric Kerridge, *passim*.

7 ibid., p.181. By "ley" is meant "land laid to grass".

8 ibid., pp.194-5, 209, 211-12, and 330-1.

9 ibid., p.256.

10 ibid., pp.37, 40 104, 194, 207, 250, 261, 272, 278, 280.

11 Robert Trow-Smith, *English Husbandry from the Earliest Times to the Present Day*, 1950, p.127.

12 A long list of references may be found in the two most comprehensive works available: Eric Kerridge, *passim*; J.D. Chambers and G.E. Mingay, *The Agricultural Revolution, 1750–1880*, 1966. A valuable summary is G.E. Mingay, "The 'Agricultural Revolution' in British History", *Agricultural History*, 1963.

13 A.H. John, "The Course of Agricultural Change", op.cit., pp.145 ff.

14 G.E. Mingay, "The Agricultural Depression", op.cit.; A.R.B. Haldane, *The Drove Roads of Scotland*, 1952; P. Mathias, "Agriculture and the Brewing and Distilling Industries in the Eighteenth Century", *Economic History Review*, 1952. The check to population growth is considered below, ch.3, pp. 53-5. On wheat prices, see above pp. 25-7 (from A.H. John, op.cit., p.172).

15 B.H. Slicher van Bath, *The Agrarian History of Western Europe, 500–1850 A.D.*, 1963, p.206.

16 Phyllis Deane, "The Output of the British Woollen Industry in the Eighteenth Century", *Journal of Economic History*, 1957, pp.221-2.

17 See Deane and Cole, op.cit., Table 17, p.65; and D.G. Barnes, *History of the English Corn Laws*, 1930, pp.14-17, and pp.30-1.

18 Kerridge, op.cit., pp.332-3.

19 Peter Mathias, *The First Industrial Nation: An Economic History of Britain, 1700–1914*, 1969, p.58; Herbert Heaton, *Economic History of Europe*, revised edition, 1963, p.410. Our italics.

20 "In fact, it is probable that too many innovations and improvements have been attributed to the famous Coke of Holkham, and too little credit has been given his predecessor, his great-uncle, Thomas Coke (Lord Lovell), 1697–1755." (Naomi Riches, *The Agricultural Revolution in Norfolk*, 1937, p.95.) "Coke's reputation as a landowner could safely have rested on his part in *introducing or disseminating knowledge of these innovations. . .*" (R.A.C. Parker, "Coke of Norfolk and the Agrarian Revolution", *Economic History Review*, 1955, p.166. Our italics.)

21 *Rural Economy*, 1770, p.315. Cf. "But, as he [Tull] mournfully says, though he grew better crops, at less cost and with greater economy of seed than his neighbours, none followed his example." (Lord Ernle, "Obstacles to Progress", in *The Land and its People*, 1925, reprinted in E.L. Jones (ed.), *Agriculture and Economic Growth*, op. cit., p.58.)

22 Naomi Riches, op.cit., pp.77, 33.

23 Lord Ernle, op.cit., p.56.

24 H. Hamilton, *The Industrial Revolution in Scotland*, 1932, pp.43, 48. Yet, "Alexander Wight had turnips as early as 1725 and was probably the first man in Scotland who raised them in drills and cultivated them by the plough." (J.E. Handley, *Scottish Farming in the Eighteenth Century*, 1953, p.149.)

25 A.H. Dodd, *The Industrial Revolution in North Wales*, second edition, 1951, p.6.
26 Deane and Cole, op.cit., p.78.
27 Professor Wilson writes: "Important as these more scientific and rational approaches to the farmer's problems were, their importance remained *qualitative rather than quantitative*." (op.cit., p.145, our italics.) Using a calculation of Mr. Fussell, Wilson estimates that imported clover seed from the main suppliers, the Low Countries, would have enabled only 4,000 acres to be sown at the end of the seventeenth century. (ibid.)
28 "To all appearances the first half of the eighteenth century was a period of depression and stagnation, broken by short outbursts of restricted progress in the spread of what were by now almost completed innovations." (E. Kerridge, op.cit., p.334.)
29 H.J. Habakkuk, "English Landownership, 1680–1740", *Economic History Review*, 1940, p.13; G.E. Mingay, *English Landed Society in the Eighteenth Century*, 1963, pp.52, 54. Dr. Kerridge is more pessimistic and refers to "a period of depressed rents that lasted approximately from 1670 to 1750". (op.cit., p.347.)
30 On "The Size of Farms in the Eighteenth Century", see the article under this title of G.E. Mingay, *Economic History Review*, 1962.
31 H.J. Habakkuk, op.cit. Professor John notes that rents increased by about 25 per cent on the Coke estate between 1718 and 1745, and also on parts of the Northumberland holdings of the Greenwich Hospital between 1735 and 1755. (op.cit., p.132.)
32 On this point, Professor Mingay has written in a private communication that: "As a background factor it might be mentioned here that the larger landowners were no longer interested in farming themselves as they had been in earlier periods. The main reason for this seems to be that profits in farming were low and too risky, and also that landowners would have had to divert capital from other uses into working capital on farms. In the landlord–tenant system the tenant normally provided all the working capital."
33 H.J. Habakkuk, op.cit.; G.E. Mingay, "An Agricultural Depression, 1730–1750", op.cit.; E.L. Jones, op.cit., especially p.160. Finance and interest rates are considered below, chapter 5, pp. 91-4.
34 Professor Jones believes higher output might well have offset the effect of falling grain prices during the early eighteenth century, but he is inclined to think even the most progressive areas in the south and east of England failed to raise output sufficiently to compensate for the fall in prices during the thirties and forties. (See E.L. Jones, op.cit., p.169.)
35 "The Agricultural Depression", op.cit., p.333.
36 "Such innovations (rotations which included root crops and artificial grasses, leys, drills, regular hoeing and weeding, and heavier manuring) were not labour-saving. . . and indeed called for more labour per acre, if not per unit of output than the old methods. . . ." (G.E. Mingay, *English Landed Society*, p.89.) See also J.D. Chambers, "Enclosure and Labour Supply in the Industrial Revolution", *Economic History Review*, 1953, pp.332-3.
37 F.J. Fisher, op.cit., p.16.
38 G.E. Mingay, op.cit., p.235.
39 Phyllis Deane, *The First Industrial Revolution*, 1967, p.43.
40 *An Economic History of England, the Eighteenth Century*, 1955, p.40. The argument needs some qualification since, as is well known, simple private agreements or collusive suits were not uncommon before the parliamentary enclosure technique was perfected in the 1760s.
41 ibid.

42 op.cit., p.256. For a wealth of information on the expenditure patterns of English noblemen, see J.H. Plumb, "The Grand Tour" and "The Noble Houses of Eighteenth-Century England", in *Men and Places*, 1966.
43 Kerridge, op.cit., chapter IV, especially pp.222, 234; Mathias, op.cit., pp.74-5.

3 THE DEMAND FOR MANUFACTURED PRODUCTS

A small fluctuation in the size of the crop built up into a wild swing in its price. Gregory King wrote that "one tenth the defect in the harvest may raise the price three tenths". Three or four years of plenty in succession left the average farmer in debt, and wiped out the small man. The thirties and forties were such a time. "Corn was so amazingly cheap in England", wrote Arthur Young, "that the nation ought never to wish to see such another period." (E.N. Williams)

From 1730 to 1756. . . complaints were incessant, through every part of the Kingdom, of the decay and ruin of manufactures. (Arthur Young)[1]

The Implications of Agricultural Prices and Output for Economic Development

The low prices of food and agricultural raw materials over 1730–50 resulted in a considerable and rather complex redistribution of the national income. The reduction in total farm income and some implications for agricultural progress were considered in the last chapter.[2] However, it is worth emphasizing here that the loss of income was borne mainly by substantial landowners and tenant farmers with large holdings; they had to dispose of the bulk of their output on depressed markets. Since it was primarily through their efforts that long-term agricultural improvements (often involving heavy investment expenditures) were achieved, the erosion of agricultural profits was particularly serious. We are not arguing here that the big landowners were so impoverished that they could not afford these expenditures. Indeed, as we have observed, some improvements had to be undertaken in order to keep the tenants on the farms. But why should the landed interest choose to make considerable long-term investments in agriculture when the prospective yields from such outlays were generally unattractive? In so far as they felt the need to economize, they probably reduced non-agricultural expenditures. For example, some big landowners might well have cancelled or scaled down their London building schemes.

We should note, again at the risk of repetition, that the loss of farm or estate income was not evenly spread across the country. While any rigid geographic demarcation cannot be entirely correct, a few writers have commented on the innovational activity in the eastern and southern regions of England with their soil and climatic advantages, and the slow progress in the west and north including Scotland and Wales. The regions which led the way in the Industrial Revolution – the north-east Midlands, Lancashire, South Wales and South Scotland – could not boast of progressive agricultures until the second half of the eighteenth century. We wonder whether the loss of income suffered by the landed interest in these regions had a retarding effect on their industrial advance. It is well known that financial capital from the agricultural sector was an important element in expenditure on canals, roads, and industrial capital after 1750/60. Admittedly much of this financial capital was channelled from the prosperous agrarian south to the industrializing north, but it is probable that during our period the landed interest in no part of the country had a significant investible surplus available for non-agrarian purposes. It was the combination of higher prices and higher output after 1750/60 which generated a large investible surplus within the agricultural sector.

The rising farm output over 1725–50 naturally had a counterpart in larger outputs of products processed from agricultural raw materials. No doubt the increased scale of these industrial activities resulted in an improved standard of living for the majority of people. Nevertheless, we agree with Dr. Clarkson's judgement: "By itself agricultural expansion in pre-industrial England did not provide a strong stimulus to economic development." This expansion led to extensive growth – i.e. more of the same. There were more wool textiles, more beer, more spirits, more starch, more candles and soap, and so on. We cannot see that this type of growth was significant in the context of Britain's overall economic development. It is the typical response of an underdeveloped country to an increase in agricultural supplies, whether temporary or permanent. Moreover, as Dr. Clarkson observes, agriculture did not usually satisfy an elastic demand, nor did it have powerful linkages with the rest of the economy (until after 1750).[3] Obviously it is no part of our argument to deny the relevance of agricultural improvement for British economic growth in the late eighteenth and nineteenth centuries. The arguments have been repeated by countless writers: it meant a smaller proportion of the work force could feed and clothe the population, a larger proportion could therefore be available for industrial activities, and more purchasing power could be generated to support manufacturing industry. But if, as before 1750, the consequence of larger supplies of agricultural raw materials was greater activity in processing them in the same ways, then – from this viewpoint – no advance was made towards the Industrial Revolution.

Those economic historians who see a considerable expansion of the British economy during our period rest their case mainly on the income-expenditure effects of the large output and low prices of farm products. This reasoning is now summarized. The income-effects were significant for three groups: the labouring people (including some craftsmen, servants, and those engaged in transport and distribution), a large number of small farmers, and wealthy landowners together with substantial freeholders and tenant farmers. Farm and industrial labourers sustained a marked increase in their real incomes. Their money incomes were higher in many instances because they worked longer hours gathering in the huge harvests, and transporting and processing the large quantities of agricultural raw materials. Some wage rates might have advanced slightly in response to the intensified demand for labour, but probably most rates remained constant.[4] Of far greater importance for the purchasing power of the labouring people was the fall in the price of food, especially bread. The real (disposable) incomes of many small farmers increased owing to larger marketable surpluses than previously (i.e. before 1730), so large as to more than offset the fall in agricultural prices and any rise in costs (e.g. through harvesting). Because of the relatively price-inelastic demand for farm products, especially grains, and also because of higher labour costs, the wealthy landowners and farmers with considerable holdings found their real incomes reduced. Since the labouring people and the poor farmers had a higher marginal propensity to consume than the wealthy landowners and substantial farmers, there was an increase in national expenditure. In so far as lower agricultural prices reflected reduced production costs following the adoption of new techniques, there occurred a rise in real disposable national income, and hence a further increase in national expenditure. The conclusion appears irresistible: higher national expenditure together with a decline in expenditure on farm products, especially bread, had their counterpart in a sustained enhanced expenditure on manufactured products. The long downward trend of agricultural prices to 1750 must have played a crucial role in the mechanics of British economic growth before the "take-off".[5]

This analysis may be challenged on the ground that less additional purchasing power (available for non-food items) was generated than might be supposed at first sight, and that higher national expenditure was diverted into channels which, on the whole, did little for economic development. It should be remembered that the price of grain was only one factor in the price of bread and other costs, for example, milling, transport and baking, would either remain about the same or move higher if bottlenecks appeared. The effect on real incomes, therefore, of the low price of grain would not be as great as is often supposed.[6] Moreover, the rise in the money incomes of the labouring people might well have been small. We must take account of attempts to economize labour and reduce wage payments. Some arable was converted to pasture; some household labour was substituted for hired hands; some labourers were presumably induced to accept a larger proportion of their pay in kind. Wage rates in a few industries might have fallen as sections of the labour market became over-supplied. This occurred when some families who derived income from both the agricultural and industrial sectors tried to offset lower income from farming by intensifying their industrial activities. A number of families, particularly in depressed agricultural areas, probably left the land and found employment elsewhere.[7] But even if their money incomes were only slightly higher, the labouring people certainly enjoyed significantly higher real incomes owing to low agricultural prices. In assessing the additional demand of the labouring poor for non-food items, we must look not at their price-elasticity of demand for the type of food which normally figured heavily in their budgets, but at their income-elasticity of demand for food in general. Whereas the former elasticity might well have been low, implying a substantial margin of surplus purchasing power, the latter was almost certainly rather high, thus implying a modest surplus. Peter Laslett has advised us to "... assume that at all times before the beginnings of industrialization a good half of those living were judged by their contemporaries to be poor, and those standards must have been harsh, even in comparison with those laid down by Victorian poor law authorities". We have Gregory King's estimate that more than half the population in 1688 consumed more than they contributed to national output, and also Colin Clark's estimate that the general living standards of the English during the late seventeenth and early eighteenth centuries were about one-third of those of the 1930s.[8] The Britain of our period falls into the high food-drain category which typifies pre-industrial societies where people in general "... behave in relation to income in ways which indicate a high income-elasticity for food, probably in the neighbourhood of unity". While this argument must not be pressed too far because poverty was not as pervasive or as severe as in many pre-industrial societies of recent history, it implies a less optimistic assessment of the extent of additional purchasing power during the 1730s and 1740s.

There are clear indications that the poor took out a large proportion of their higher standard of living by purchasing relatively more expensive food and drink. The heavy consumption of gin between about 1724 and 1751, especially in London, has been stressed by many writers. The output of spirits exceeded 8 million gallons in 1742/3, this representing about a fivefold increase since the beginning of the century. Dr. Gilboy has stressed the addiction of Londoners to gin: "For some thirty years the surplus (of Londoners) was apparently spent in gin, but after that other commodities of a more healthy nature took their place in the budget." By the middle of the century, according to Dr. Dorothy Davis, ". . . about one house in fifteen in London. . . was a public house of some sort". Professor Ashton has reminded us that gin addiction became serious not only in London but in ". . . the other large towns. . . (and) there is evidence that the country districts were also affected". And this was also the view of Professor Lecky: ". . . it was not till about 1724 that the passion for gin-drinking appears to have infected the masses of the population, and it spread with the rapidity and violence of an epidemic. . ." The thirty-year gin mania was brought to an end by the Act of 1751 which prohibited retail sales by distillers and sharply lifted spirit taxes and licence fees.[10]

Many writers have commented on the gradual substitution of bread made from wheat- rather than coarse-grain flour. By 1748, Londoners rarely ate other than wheat-grain bread.[11] The prices of meat and dairy products fell less precipitously than those of grains, and this may be explained by the desire for more expensive, palatable foods and for a more varied diet. Sugar and tea had become near-necessities in parts of England by the mid-eighteenth century. The point is underlined by a quotation from a contemporary cited by Professor Chambers:

> . . . written in 1739 by a doctor of some distinction . . . "People here are not without their Tea, Coffee, and Chocolate, especially the first, the Use which is spread to that Degree, that not only Gentry and Wealthy Travellers drink it constantly, but almost every Seamer, Sizer and Winder will have her Tea in a Morning. . . and even a common Washerwoman thinks she has not had a proper Breakfast without Tea and hot buttered White Bread . . . I could not forbear looking earnestly and with some Degree of Indignation at a ragged and

> greasy creature who came into a Shop with her two Children and asked for a Pennyworth of Tea and halfpenny worth of sugar. . . and said she could not live without drinking tea every day." (From Dr. Deering's *History of Nottingham*, cited J.D. Chambers, "Vale of Trent, 1670–1800", p.24.)

Luxury imports of the seventeenth century had come within the reach of all but the desperately poor before 1750. Thus Professor Davis writes: "The great expanding imports were colonial sugar, tobacco, rice, coffee and other foods and drinks, and these flooded in, despite the duties. . . Demand curves were shifting under the influence of changes in incomes and tastes. . . Duties and the changes in them imposed no check; the consumer paid what he was asked."[12] There seems little doubt then that food and drink provided a considerable outlet for any surplus purchasing power of the labouring people.

Apart from food and drink, there were other forms in which the labouring poor took out their higher living standards. No doubt tobacco (again probably for some a near-necessity by the mid-century) and processed agricultural raw materials, especially wool textiles and better boots and shoes, had a strong claim on any additional purchasing power.[13] And there is evidence that more was spent on amusement, for example going to fairs. But the real incomes of the labouring poor could hardly have stretched much further. It is well known, of course, that many contemporaries boasted of the affluence of the English poor compared with their European counterparts. Our period was not exceptional in this respect, the same comparison having been made over the two previous centuries.[14] The comparison, whenever made, is consistent with either economic development or deceleration. Clearly the additional expenditure of the poor in our period resulted in an expansion of industrial activities such as distilling, sugar-refining, food- and tobacco-processing, and cloth-making. We cannot be sure whether this expansion was quicker or slower after about 1725. However, apart from the larger production units which became more common in the brewing and distillery industries, it was an expansion associated with little innovational activity. Consequently, given near-stagnation in agriculture, the increase in these industrial activities gave every promise of not being maintained once the years of exceptionally low food prices ended. We conclude that the expenditure of the labouring poor could not have formed a base for general or permanent industrial development during the second quarter of the eighteenth century.

On turning our attention to the income-elasticities of the middle classes, we find ourselves on more treacherous ground. To some extent, and particularly for the less prosperous groups, we should expect their spending priorities to be similar to those of the poor with an emphasis on food, drink, tobacco and apparel. The middle classes were characterized by their habits of conspicuous consumption and their desire to "ape their betters". We must suppose then that they bought *inter alia* more expensive clothing, leather-ware, wigs, trinkets and jewellery. There was an increased demand for services, especially from the upper middle class: they hired more servants, travelled more, made more frequent visits to the theatre and to London, and mixed more with their superiors at famous spas such as Bath and Cheltenham. Undeniably the additional purchasing power of both the labouring and middle classes resulted in *some* increased sales of a wide variety of some if not of all industrial products, including furniture, pottery, metal- and glass-wares, and so on. But we emphasize that the redistribution of national income was heavily weighted in favour of the poor and, to a smaller degree, the lower middle class. Given their likely income-elasticities and some of the likely uses to which the middle class as a whole put their higher real incomes, we cannot believe a tenable case can be made on the basis of low agricultural prices for the view that manufacturing industry in general was stimulated by high levels of expenditure, or that the pattern of additional expenditure was significant for the progress of the British economy towards the Industrial Revolution.

The Influence of Other Factors on Economic Development

The demand for manufactured goods during the second quarter of the eighteenth century was adversely affected by the attitude of labour to work, a demographic pause, and government economic policies. The case for retarded economic growth has been strengthened by the writings of contemporaries who stressed the high leisure-preference and the truculence of labour; and there were complaints too of what is now called absenteeism. Lewis Paul's complaint about his London labourers in 1742 was not untypical: "I have not half my people come to work today, and I have no great fascination in the prospect I have to put myself in the power of such people."[15] Professor John has tried to play down the importance of leisure-preference in the following passage:

In the first place, the age structure of the population meant that a

> substantial part of the labour force comprised either apprentices or indoor servants, and for these the chances of idling were more limited than for the outdoor worker. . . Secondly, preference for leisure was countered by sharp increases in wages during the seasonal rushes of work which were so marked a feature of pre-industrial economies. . . Thirdly, there is evidence of a good deal of migration, both seasonal and permanent, to areas of growing activity, suggesting that expanding sectors, whether in agriculture or industry, obtained at least part of their additional labour requirements.

Nevertheless, John prefaces these remarks with the concession that ". . . there were doubtless many who had a high leisure-preference".[16]

The strength of market forces in combating a high leisure-preference might be questioned. We cannot exclude the possibility of a tendency towards a lagged and conceivably perverse effect. Thus labourers who were induced to work even longer and harder than usual might have taken life even more easily than usual afterwards. Given the harsh and short lives to which the vast majority were condemned, the marginal disutility of labour must have been very high. Peter Laslett, in what has been described as his "moving requiem" for the world we have lost, has written: "The working of the land, the labour in the craftsman's shop, were infinitely taxing. The surviving peasantry in Western Europe still shock us with their worn hands and faces, their immeasurable fatigue."[17] The shortage of coins for wage payments might well have reinforced the tendency towards a high leisure-preference. Certainly as the century wore on, more and more industrialists became convinced that workers should have more purchasing power in the form of money (either of the realm or locally made). An associated point and another reason for an inelastic or backward-sloping labour-supply curve are provided by Bishop Berkeley who wondered (in 1755) ". . . whether the creating of wants be not the likeliest way to produce industry in people". We might infer from this statement that few or not many new or improved cheap products become available during the thirties and forties.[18] Furthermore, long drinking sessions in gin palaces and public houses must have resulted in some forced leisure-preference and impaired labour productivity.

Militating against incentive payments to labour were the settlement laws and the mercantilist doctrine favouring low wages. Even though the settlement laws were not strictly enforced, the effect on the mobility of labour before the Industrial Revolution should not be underestimated or ignored. However, we do not wish to press this point as far as Adam

Smith who wrote: "There is scarce a poor man in England, of forty years of age . . . who has not, in some part of his life, felt himself most cruelly oppressed by this ill-contrived law of settlements." Although two contemporaries, Dr. Burn and Mr. Hay, agreed with Smith's view, others were more moderate in their assessment. The settlement laws were not a dead letter, and the movement of labour was in some measure restricted by them.[19] Finally, there can be no doubt that many employers and JPs continued to be influenced by the mercantilist view that wages should be low and pressures to raise them resisted. It is well known that the Statute of Artificers (1563) gave JPs the power to assess wages – i.e. to fix maximum wage rates, but historians are not agreed on the extent to which this practice was breaking down in the eighteenth century. J. Thorold Rogers, for example, fiercely contends ". . . that from 1563 to 1824 (the year the Combination Acts were repealed) a conspiracy. . . was entered into to cheat the English workman of his wages, to deprive him of hope, and to degrade him into irremediable poverty". But let us give the last word to Arthur Young: "Everyone but an idiot knows that the lower classes must be kept poor or they will never be industrious. I do not mean that the poor in England are to be kept like the poor of France; but the state of the country considered, they must be (like all mankind) in poverty or they will not work."[20]

Many historians have drawn attention to the check to population growth between 1720 and 1750. Using Brownlee's estimates for England and Wales, Cole and Deane find that, with 1781 = 100, the population index moves from 80 in 1721 to 79 in 1731 and 1741, and then reaches 82 in 1751.[21] Table 1 provides some measure of population change for England and Wales in the eighteenth century. However, recent research on parish registers suggests that the population was 5.2 million or less in 1695, and that it grew rapidly between 1690 and 1720 (far more so than the table indicates) – probably at a rate similar to that experienced over 1750–80. This is consistent with the hypothesis tentatively advanced by Professor Tucker. He sees the higher demógraphic growth rate between 1750 and 1780 firstly as a reaction to the abnormally low rate between 1720 and 1750, and secondly as a resumption of the secular rate which can be traced from the sixteenth century if not from the Black Death (1348/49). The period from the end of the seventeenth to the mid-eighteenth century witnessed two sub-periods of population expansion: 1695–1720 and 1740–50, the last decade (especially from 1745) being chiefly a recovery phase after the demographic reverses of the twenties and thirties. Population downturns occurred in a number of years between

Table 1: Population Estimates

Year	Millions
1701	5.83
1711	5.98
1721	6.00
1731	5.95
1741	5.93
1751	6.14
1761	6.57
1771	7.05
1781	7.53
1791	8.25
1801	9.16

Source: Deane and Cole, op.cit., p.6.

1718 and 1741, mortality peaks being registered in 1719, 1727–9, 1736, and 1740–1. They were occasioned not by the plague, whose last visitation was in 1665, but by epidemics, particularly smallpox, typhus and influenza.[22]

The main demographic features of our period are highlighted by the work of regional historians. Probably the only part of the country to enjoy a continuous advance in population was the north-western counties of England. For Nottingham and Nottinghamshire, Professor Chambers sees a rising population from 1690 to 1720 with a definite pause over the next twenty-five to thirty-five years. The epidemic of 1727–30 was disastrous, and recovery was slow because of further epidemics in 1736, 1741–2, and 1747–8. Dr. Eversley emphasizes the high mortality rate over the decade 1725–34 experienced by a number of Worcestershire villages, a rate which Professor Krause notes ". . . is above the Indian rate of 1911–21, when the great influenza epidemic struck". The worst years, according to Eversley, were 1725–29 when the death rate exceeded 65 per thousand compared with the early eighteenth-century rate of a shade below 30 per thousand. Dr. Tranter in his report on thirty Bedfordshire villages notes the bad epidemic years of 1727–30, 1740–2, and 1747–8. Both he and Eversley tell us that the population levels of 1725 were not regained until the early fifties. After examining the records of two hundred widely scattered villages in England, Krause reports high death rates for much of the second quarter of the eighteenth century.

the rates over 1725–9 probably being the highest of the century. All these findings are similar to those of Dorothy George in her account of demographic change in London.[23]

We must now ask why the check to population growth was a major cause of economic deceleration during our period. A rising population tended to stimulate economic activity through a larger work force and increasing needs to be satisfied. It was not Thomas Malthus but Adam Smith who understood the importance of population, for he had no reservations when he wrote: "The most decisive mark of the prosperity of any nation is the increase in the number of its inhabitants."[24] The demographic reverses between 1720 and 1750 were a significant factor in the weaker demand for farm products. The deceleration or stagnation in the agricultural sector was at least in part the outcome of the failure of population to grow at the pre-1700 or pre-1720 rate. And paradoxically low prices of farm products reduced the birth rate via the marriage rate. When farmers' incomes were low, they preferred unmarried labourers who lived in to married cottage labourers who required higher incomes for subsistence. "As Arthur Young said again and again, it was cottage labour that raised the birth rate, and the difficulties of farmers and landlords in these years would not encourage the building of cottages."[25] The causal link between population change and agricultural prices ran both ways. Moreover, we must assume that the economic horizons of entrepreneurs narrowed in times of epidemics and shorter life expectancy. And the higher death rate surely reinforced leisure-preference and gin addiction, the latter carrying the death rate even higher and probably lowering the birth rate through reduced fertility. Just as the steady and cumulative increase of population from about 1750 is usually regarded as a most significant causal factor in the British "take-off", we contend here that the expansion of demand for manufactured products during the late seventeenth and early eighteenth century probably slackened during our period in sympathy with the reduced rate of population growth.

The economic policies of Robert Walpole, 1721 to 1742, were designed for commercial rather than industrial expansion. At the end of the long European conflict in 1713, British foreign trade was subject to a heavy tax burden, duties being levied on nearly all imports and exports. Nevertheless, commerce was big business:

> When the Georgian period opened, the merchants were the driving force of the English economy. . . . Their agents were importing iron from

> Sweden, tea from China, and sugar from the West Indies. They bought tobacco in Virginia and sold it in Moscow; and they sold English cloth in the four corners of the earth. They had their irons in every fire; they controlled the Bank of England, they victualled the army and navy, they lent money to the government. . .[26]

Walpole aimed at making this scenario even more dazzling for, between 1721 and 1724, he abolished most export duties and abolished or reduced import duties on raw materials. This policy undoubtedly strengthened Britain's position as a trading and carrying nation. However, we should note that commercial prosperity was not accompanied by a substantial growth of imports or manufactured exports (net of re-exports which accounted for about 30 per cent of total exports during the first three-quarters of the eighteenth century). On index (1772/3 = 100), imports rose from 34 in 1702/3 to 52 in 1722/3, and then only to 59 in 1742/3, and only to 66 in 1752/3. This slow upward movement was all the more remarkable in view of Walpole's tariff reforms: imported raw materials were cheaper, and presumably there was some substitution of legal trading for smuggling. The most obvious explanation is a far from buoyant level of domestic expenditure. Moving to the export scene, we have Professor Davis's report: "The eighteenth century was by no means a long success story for English merchants that its predecessor had been. It was a century of realignment of trade – geographically and in terms of commodities – and not until towards the mid-century could the swelling tide be seen unmistakably rolling again."[27]

In his account of the history of Liverpool, Professor Hyde writes enthusiastically of the town's development from the 1660s. By the early eighteenth century, her export trade was considerable in a wide variety of products including salt, textiles, pottery, refined sugar, leather goods, metal-wares, glass and coal. Landowners' income flowed into commerce, especially between 1680 and 1715. Down to the early twenties, much effort was expended in improving communications by road and river from Liverpool to a number of towns in northern England. But then the pace of advance apparently slackened. "If one takes the tonnage of shipping entering and clearing the port between 1716 and 1744, there is a surprisingly low annual rate of growth of 0.7 per cent. . . . After 1750, however, the growth of a large import trade, coupled with improved communications with the expanding industrial activity in the hinterland, led to a re-adjustment of motivating influences."[28]

In fostering the interests of the merchant class, Walpole brought them continued and unprecedented prosperity. His emphasis on trade has been interpreted by at least one writer as a change in economic philosophy. "Economic mercantilism was indeed a declining force after 1720. Walpole cleared away all export duties, and Hume suggested in 1740 that Britain might even benefit from Continental prosperity. Trade, not mere bullion, came to be regarded as the chief source of the nation's wealth."[29] In any case, the profitability of commerce was in sharp contrast with that of agriculture and industry. We have already stressed the lack of inducement to long-term investment in agriculture, and arguments have been advanced in this chapter for supposing that the demand for manufactured products was not high. Furthermore, the collapse of the South Sea Bubble and the Bubble Act of 1720 which made shareholders liable "to their last acre and penny" must have undermined the confidence of potential investors in industry. In these circumstances, and given the substantial capital requirements of commerce, it seems certain that long-term capital requirements of commerce, it seems certain that long-term investible funds were diverted away from both agriculture and industry towards commerce. Commerce, in brief, offered a larger and safer return; commercial rather than industrial capitalism was the order of the day.[30] We agree with the assessment of Arthur Innis: "He (Walpole) raised the country to an unparalleled pitch of commercial prosperity. . . The country settled down to a career of commercial prosperity. . . *but the conditions of her progress had not radically altered*."[31] We conclude therefore that foreign trade data and commercial policy support the view we are defending.

Walpole aimed for an export- and re-export-orientated industrial expansion. He favoured cheap raw materials and cheap labour, but it was no part of his policy to generate a strong home demand for manufactured products. The excise, i.e. the duty levied on home consumers of home-produced goods, had been introduced by John Pym in 1643. It had been extended to more and more commodities, especially as a means of raising revenue in wartime. The period 1697 to 1712 saw many additions to the list of commodities subject to this tax – e.g. malt, candles, hops, hides, water-borne coal, soap, paper, starch, printed textile fabrics (calicoes), hackney-chairs, cards and dice. The excise, of course, was regressive in the sense that it bore most heavily on those least able to bear it, the poor. Their purchasing power was significantly eroded by the excise but Walpole, on coming to power in 1721, was convinced that no fairer tax could be devised than one levied on general expenditure. Indeed, to quote the Treasurer himself: "As to the manner of raising taxes upon the people, it is a certain maxim that that tax which is the most equal and the most general is the most just and least burdensome."[32] Import duties on raw materials and export duties were undesirable because their incidence was not general. The land tax was unfair because its burden fell on one section of the community. He therefore reduced it from four to two shillings in the pound. He saw nothing inequitable in reducing it further to one shilling in 1732, making up the revenue by reviving the salt tax which had been abolished two years previously. Under his administration and throughout our period, the tax system was clearly regressive, the excise being the chief form of national revenue. Many commodities were taxed, including such popular consumer goods as beer, spirits, tea, coffee, chocolate and tobacco. The tax on malt and beer alone raised one-quarter of national revenue in the thirties. Admittedly Walpole shifted his ground during the battle over the Excise Bill in 1733, and came to see that a general excise was regressive, but his conversion appears to have been far from complete. Table 2 shows that, on the eve of war in 1739, more than half the national revenue was raised through the excise. Additional taxes were raised during the hostilities, for example, on glass and coaches in 1746.[33] We believe the gains in real income of the poor and, to a smaller extent, the middle class through lower agricultural prices were reduced by the fiscal policy of Walpole.

Table 2: Revenue from Taxes, 1739

Land tax at 2s. in pound	£1,000,000
Window tax and tax on pensions	£ 135,000
Customs	£1,400,000
Excise	£3,000,000
Stamps	£ 150,000

Source: Stephen Dowell, *History of Taxation*, 1884, p.109.

1 E.N. Williams, *Life in Georgian England*, 1962, p.65; Arthur Young, *Political Arithmetic*, 1774, p.32, cited by J.D. Chambers, "Vale of Trent, 1670–1800", op.cit., p.46. Readers who might see merit in a mathematical approach to the subject matter of this chapter should consult R.A. Ippolito, "The Effect of the Agricultural Depression on Industrial Demand in England, 1730–1750", *Economica*, 1975.
2 See above, chapter 2, pp. 33-8.
3 L.A. Clarkson, op.cit., p.73.

4 Adam Smith observed that wages did not change with the price of food. "These vary everywhere from year to year, frequently from month to month. But in many places the price of labour remains uniformly the same for half a century together." (The Wealth of Nations, Book I, chapter VIII.) The work of Dr. E.W. Gilboy supports this view. See her *Wages in Eighteenth-Century England,* 1934, Appendix II. Both references are cited by T.S. Ashton, *An Economic History of England,* pp.219-20.

5 T.S. Ashton, op.cit., pp.55-6, 60-3, 205; and *Economic Fluctuations in England, 1700–1800,* chapter II, especially pp.40-7; A.H. John, "Agricultural Productivity and Economic Growth", and E.L. Jones, "Agriculture and Economic Growth in England", in E.L. Jones (ed.), op.cit., pp.170-3. On some theoretical aspects of the subject matter of this section, see J.D. Gould, "Agricultural Fluctuations and the English Economy in the Eighteenth Century", *Journal of Economic History,* 1962.

6 I am indebted to Professors Coats and Mingay for this point.

7 The worsted section of the hosiery industry provides a good example of an over-supplied labour market. Cf. "At this epoch, 1740 to 1750, the wages for making the common kinds of hose were reduced very low; and many of the parish apprentices, ill managed, ill taught, and little cared for, were reduced almost to starvation." W. Felkin, *History of the Machine-Wrought Hosiery and Lace Manufactures.* 1867, centenary edition 1967, p.82.

8 T.P.R. Laslett, *The World We Have Lost,* 1965, p.45; Gregory King, *General Account,* 1690; Colin Clark, *The Conditions of Economic Progress,* 1940, pp.41, 83.

9 T.W. Schultz, *The Economic Organization of Agriculture,* 1953, pp.32, 44.

10 Gilboy, op.cit., p.222; Davis, *Fairs, Shops and Supermarkets,* 1966, p.213 (basing herself on W. Maitland, *History and Survey of London,* 1756, pp.719, 735); Ashton, *An Economic History of England,* p.7; W.E.H. Lecky, *A History of England in the Eighteenth Century,* 1878, vol. II, pp.101-4.

11 Peter Kalm, *Visit to England,* 1748, pp.55, 88.

12 R. Davis, "The Rise of Protection in England, 1689–1786", *Economic History Review,* 1966, p.315.

13 It is clear from Eden's *The State of the Poor,* 1797 (based on information collected from across the country over 1794–6) that an increase in income was quickly reflected in higher expenditure on boots and clothing. Dr. Clarkson has expressed the opinion in a private letter that the price- and income-elasticity of demand for boots and shoes were not high, except at the lowest levels of income. Hence people tended to purchase better boots and shoes.
Moreover, the output of leather varied little during the period under review.

14 L.A. Clarkson, op.cit., pp.10-11.

15 Cited by T.S. Ashton, op.cit., p.211. On the opinions of contemporaries, see A.W. Coats, "Changing Attitudes to Labour in the Mid-Eighteenth Century", *Economic History Review,* 1958.

16 A.H. John, op.cit., pp.175-6.

17 Ibid., pp.28-9.

18 T.S. Ashton, op.cit., pp.213-14.

19 On Smith's and some other views, see J.L. and Barbara Hammond, *The Village Labourer,* pp.88-96.

20 Gilboy, *passim;* R.K. Kelsall, *Wage Regulation under the Statute of Artificers,* 1938; J. Thorold Rogers, *Six Centuries of Work and Wages,* 1909 edition, p.398; Young, *Eastern Tour,* 1771, vol. IV, pp.360-2.
In a private letter, Professor Coats writes: "On the whole I do feel that the pre-1750 period was dominated by low-wage attitudes, and one in which high leisure-preferences were significant." And, as Professor Chambers has observed,

". . . there was. . . a constant pressure for higher wages; but paradoxically, owing to an absence of a conception of rising living standards through earning power alone, there was a marked preference for leisure over harder work for higher earnings". (*Population, Economy, and Society in Pre-Industrial England*, 1972, p.140.) On the other hand, Dr. Clarkson tells us people wished to acquire new goods to satisfy new wants, and hence leisure-preference was not high. Again, he points to the high-wage doctrine of some economic writers. (op.cit., pp.43-4.) The reader is left to draw his own conclusions, especially with regard to the period under review.

21 W.A. Cole and Phyllis Deane, "The Growth of National Incomes", in H.J. Habakkuk and M. Postan (eds.), *The Cambridge Economic History of Europe*, 1965, vol. VI, p.8.

22 J.D. Chambers, *Population in Pre-Industrial England*, pp.112-15, 23, 32; G.S.L. Tucker, "English Pre-Industrial Population Trends", *Economic History Review*, 1963.

23 J.D. Chambers, op.cit., pp.62-3, 94, 148; and "Vale of Trent", p.4; D.E.C. Eversley, "A Survey of Population in an Area of Worcestershire from 1660 to 1850, on the Basis of Parish Registers", in D.V. Glass and D. Eversley (eds.), *Population in History*, 1965; N.L. Tranter, "Demographic Change in Bedfordshire 1670–1800", unpublished Ph.D. thesis, University of Nottingham, 1966 (cited by J.D. Chambers); J.T. Krause, "Some Aspects of Population Change, 1690–1790", in E.L. Jones and G.E. Mingay (eds.), *Land, Labour and Population in the Industrial Revolution*, 1967; M.D. George, "Some Causes of the Increase of Population in the Eighteenth Century as Illustrated by London", *Economic Journal*, 1922.

24 *The Wealth of Nations*, vol. I, chapter VIII.

25 J.D. Chambers, "Vale of Trent", pp.44-5. See also his *Population in Pre-Industrial England*, p.118.

26 E.N. Williams, op. cit., pp.55-6.

27 R.Davis, "English Foreign Trade, 1700–1774", *Economic History Review*, 1962, p.285. Import statistics from Deane and Cole, op.cit., Table 13, p.44.

28 F.E. Hyde, *Liverpool and the Mersey*, 1971, especially pp.8-9, 12-15, 23-4.

29 G.B. Hertz, *The Old Colonial System*, 1905, p.38.

30 "Industries other than shipping and those associated with colonial trade were relatively starved of capital by the navigation system, until by the mid-eighteenth century England had so far surpassed the Netherlands that Dutch capital was pouring into England." (Christopher Hill, *Reformation to Industrial Revolution*, op.cit., p.128.)

31 Arthur D. Innis, *Britain and Her Rivals in the Eighteenth Century, 1713-1789*, 1895, pp.173, 181. The last words quoted, not italicized in the original, are more than a hint that Innis did not equate commercial prosperity with economic growth.

32 N.A. Briscoe, *The Economic Policy of Robert Walpole*, 1907, p.88, citing *Hansard*, vol. III, p.944.

33 On the economic philosophy of Walpole, see Briscoe, op.cit., especially pp.129-30, 177. Information on the excise has been obtained from Stephen Dowell, *History of Taxation*, 1884, p.11; T.S. Ashton, *Economic Fluctuations*, p.28; Briscoe, op.cit., p.63; Christopher Hill, op.cit., p.180.

4 THE INDUSTRIAL SECTOR

> There was a real industrial recovery after the end of the wars in 1713, but it was brought to an end by the depression that burst the South Sea Bubble. My impression is that there was some recovery from the mid-twenties which may have been slowed by the continental wars of the thirties and certainly in most industries by the longer war in which Britain participated in 1739–48. The boom of the late forties was a post-war boom with the release of much demand that had been built up for a long time; much of the earlier stagnation had been associated with war in England and in Europe. (Ralph Davis)

> Economic "growth" in this sense of differentiation – structural change, "deepening" of investment, technical change involving a change in "production functions" – has to be distinguished from economic "expansion" – extending a traditional pattern of economic activity without such qualitative changes. . . . Britain saw the beginning of such a process between the 1740s and the 1780s. (P. Mathias)[1]

Introduction

We now support the case for economic deceleration over 1725–50 by reviewing some of the more important features and developments in a number of secondary industries, postponing to the next chapter consideration of the extractive industries, iron, transport, and the building industry. In both chapters we shall find evidence for the view that a high general level of demand was not generated by low agricultural prices. Not only did output of some industries stagnate, but profit margins appear on the whole to have been under pressure. We shall note other disturbing features which suggest a slowing down or a check to overall expansion of the British economy. In some industries the pace of advance in terms of output and/or technology from the late seventeenth and early eighteenth century seems not to have been maintained during our period. Expansion often took the form of a larger output produced within the traditional or established industrial framework or structure, from which we may infer little change in production functions and a widening rather than a deepening of the capital structure.

In other words, methods of production were more or less the same after 1725 as before and, to the extent that capital accumulation took place it usually consisted of duplicating – sometimes with slight modifications – existing types of equipment. There are examples of entrepreneurial failure to innovate or overcome bottlenecks. The performance of industries central to the Industrial Revolution was unspectacular, and certainly failed to foreshadow the "take-off". In short, on the sides of both demand and supply, we shall discover strong grounds for the contention that our period witnessed a pause in economic growth.

Textiles and Hosiery

The textile and hosiery industries as a group continued to represent a very large part of all industrial activities. Hoffmann's calculations suggest that cloth accounted for about a third of the net value of manufactured output in our period.[2] Table 3 is reproduced from Miss Deane's well-known article, and it clearly indicates the small increase in incomes earned from manufacturing wool textiles between 1695 and 1741, and the very much larger increase afterwards down to 1772.

Table 3: Estimated Growth of the Woollen Manufacture in England and Wales in the Eighteenth Century

Circa	Wool consumed (including imports) millions of pounds (lb.)	Value added in manufacture £ millions	Value of final product £ millions
1695	40	3.0	5.0
1741	57	3.6	5.1
1772	85	7.0	10.2

Source: Phyllis Deane, "The Output of the British Woollen Industry in the Eighteenth Century", *Journal of Economic History* 1957, p.220.

There is strong evidence that, in the case of the wool textile industry, deceleration had set in by the turn of the eighteenth century. Demand from both home and oversea markets failed to match the increase in supply and, as we have already observed, the price of wool was on a downward trend from the early 1660s to 1742. Many governments succumbed to pressure to pass measures aimed at helping the wool textile industry. We have mentioned attempts to boost exports such as the ban on Irish exports (1699), the abolition of the duty on wool textile exports (1700) and the Methuen Treaty (1703).[3] Other measures included the Acts of 1678 and 1680 which made it compulsory to bury the dead in a woollen shroud and the famous Act of 1721 which prohibited the import of printed calicoes. But apparently nothing could stem the withering profitability of the industry. Pamphleteers were active in the 1730s complaining of its depressed state. And when war began in 1739, exports of wool textiles declined sharply, and showed little recovery before the mid-forties.[4] The considerable buyer resistance in overseas markets together with wartime trading difficulties were all the more serious because wool textiles were still at that time the most important single export, and Britain needed foreign exchange in order to buy increasing quantities of raw materials to widen her industrial base. We agree with Miss Deane's verdict:

> The immense importance of the tropical commodities lay in the fact that they increased British purchasing power on the continent of Europe. Britain needed her European imports for vital productive purposes and not merely to meet the upper-class demand for wine and brandy. She needed foreign timber, pitch and hemp for her ships and buildings, high-grade bar iron for her metal trades, raw and thrown silk for her textile trades. *Her industrial expansion along traditional lines was severely restricted by the fact that the demand for woollen products was inelastic and already near saturation point in traditional markets.*[5]

By the early eighteenth century at the latest, the wool textile industry was characterized by an imbalance between spinning and weaving activities. The loom had been so much improved that the work of several spinners was needed to keep a weaver fully occupied. In the event, the shortage of yarn was not alleviated until the appearance of James Hargreaves' spinning-jenny in the mid- to late sixties. But the need for such an invention, which multiplied the output of a spinner many times, had been urgent for decades. The wool textile industry in our period continued to suffer from this major bottleneck, and it is a good example of a traditional industry whose expansion occurred within a long-established structure. When all these considerations are taken into account, the growth of the country's premier industry looks unimpressive in the context of the overall development of the British economy.

The linen industry was encouraged by William and Mary who

incorporated three joint-stock companies in England, Scotland and Ireland mainly to stimulate the introduction of superior French methods of damask and linen weaving.[6] The next major technical advance came in 1749 when Dr. Roebuck began producing sulphuric acid at Prestonpans and thereby revolutionized the bleaching process. There are conflicting estimates of the growth of the English branch of the industry. Deane and Cole see a slow rise of output, perhaps from 21 to 26 million yards between 1730 and 1754. Dr. Harte believes output might have doubled in the second quarter of the century but, on his calculations, much of this increase occurred in the 1740s.[7] Under the 1727 Act, the Scottish linen industry was given financial assistance: flax-growing was subsidized, spinning schools were established, and attempts were made to improve the standard of weaving. Consequently, output increased from a little over 2 to 7½ million yards between 1728 and 1750. Although this rise in the output of cloth undoubtedly accounted in large measure for the higher Scottish standard of living over this period, producers both north and south of the border encountered stiffer market conditions, particularly during the thirties and early forties. Parliament finally yielded to numerous requests for further assistance, and the Bounty Acts of 1742 and 1745 were passed. From 1743 an export subsidy of between 8 and 16 per cent was applied to the coarsest types of material. However, this proved insufficient and an additional 4 to 10 per cent was granted together with another subsidy of 12 to 14 per cent on some better materials.[8] It seems more than likely that low profitability was a feature of not only the wool textile but also the linen industry.

We turn next to the cotton textile industry which was to some extent linked with the linen industry since cotton and linen yarn were woven into fustians. It is well known that the cotton textile industry was given an unintentional stimulus by the Calicoe Act of 1721 (to which we have already referred).[9] Yet, as can be deduced from Table 4, it remained small in size and slow in expansion until the third quarter of the eighteenth century. As late as 1761, Dr. Lilley assures us, ". . . the Manchester cotton industry had been so unimportant that there were no cotton workers in a procession representing the principal traders of the city; by 1774 there were 30,000 people in the industry in or near Manchester".[10] It is not without significance that John Kay's fly-shuttle, patented in 1733 and known and used in Lancashire and Yorkshire by 1737, made little headway down to the sixties, despite its potential for cutting the labour cost of weaving by up to 50 per cent. Although the invention threatened to accentuate the shortage of yarn, it was only later that the

Table 4: Average Annual Consumption of Cotton in Great Britain (after deduction for exports)

Years	Cotton Wool (lb. millions)
1721–1730	1.5
1731–1740	1.7
1741–1750	2.1
1751–1760	2.8
1761–1770	3.7
1771–1780	5.1

Source: A.P. Wadsworth and J. de L. Mann, *The Cotton Trade and Industrial Lancashire, 1660–1780*, Manchester, 1931 (reprinted 1965), p.170.

aggravated disequilibrium between the spinning and weaving sections of the industry induced improved methods of spinning.[11]

The hosiery industry was incorporated by Oliver Cromwell, and its status was recognized by the government of Charles II in 1664. From the beginning the main centres of the industry were to be found in London and the north-east Midlands, at first in Nottinghamshire but spreading into neighbouring Leicestershire and Derbyshire. The growth of the industry in these three counties can be gauged by the increase in the number of knitting-frames from 140 in 1664 to 3,500 in 1727. For the country as a whole, the number of frames increased over the same period from 600 to 8,000. But the pace of advance slackened during the second quarter of the eighteenth century. While the number of frames in Nottinghamshire and Leicestershire rose to more than 4,000, the industry in Derbyshire was in decline and, according to Dr. Dearing, "what remained of the London manufacture [in 1751 when he wrote] did 'hardly deserve the name of trade' ".[12] There is good evidence that all sections of the industry – silk, woollen (and worsted), and cotton – passed through a difficult phase in the thirties and forties.

Until the latter part of the seventeenth century, the industry concentrated almost exclusively on satisfying the market for silk hose, waistcoats, and other luxury garments. It was a fashion industry based on London. Despite the high cost of the frame and the need to import silk, output grew vigorously from the 1660s. Silk manufacturing flourished in the late seventeenth and early eighteenth century mainly as a result of the immigration of skilled Huguenot weavers in and after 1685 and also the ban on imported Indian silks effective from 1699. This branch of the hosiery industry reached a high point in 1718 when Thomas Lombe established his Derby factory, the first mechanized factory driven by water power. It will be recalled that he installed silk-throwing machinery, and was highly successful because he undersold Italian silks by a substantial margin.[13] It seems, however, that the profits of some manufacturers might have been falling by about 1720 because they joined wool textile manufacturers in pressing Parliament to pass the Calicoe Act of 1721. Admittedly Lombe amassed a fortune of about £120,000 between 1718 and 1732, but it should be remembered he held a patent for the silk-throwing device over these years. The failure of his enterprise soon after his patent expired in 1732 was not only a major setback for this branch of the industry but suggests his counterparts had ceased to thrive before that date. Import statistics for silk indicate a slow growth down to 1740, after which they fall to a level lower even than that recorded at the beginning of the eighteenth century.[14] The fortunes of silk manufacturers did not revive until the fifties when factories were built in Stockport, Congleton, Macclesfield, Sheffield and Watford. For whatever reasons, the silk manufacturing industry suffered a reverse during the period under review, only to expand afterwards using the throwing principle adopted by Lombe.

The woollen, worsted and cotton sections of the hosiery industry located themselves mainly around Nottingham and Leicester. The demand for cheap hosiery and the attraction of a market less susceptible to the dictates of fashion were major factors responsible for their expanding output in the last years of the seventeenth and the first years of the eighteenth century. Although the industry centred on Nottingham and Leicester continued to grow during the first half of the eighteenth century, it certainly did not prosper for much of the period from 1720 to 1750. Its growth was partly associated with an intensified demand for cheaper varieties of hose and partly with the transfer of frames from London by master hosiers who were attracted by the low cost of living, the low cost of labour, and its availability. Professor Chambers reports: "Between 1732 and 1750, 800 frames were brought from London to Nottingham and sold for less than half price and a similar number to Leicester, whilst numbers were laid up as useless or sold for old iron." As for woollen and linen cloths, demand lagged behind supply: home demand was far from buoyant, and great difficulty was experienced in competing in the only expanding export market, the American colonies, against the more efficient industry of Saxony. The hosiers and framework-knitters of Leicester petitioned Parliament for relief in 1738;

the phrase 'as poor as a stockinger' was frequently heard in the forties, and the widespread poverty of the industry was manifested in the parliamentary inquiry of 1753. Not only were real wages very low, possibly near starvation levels for many workers in the forties, but the Framework Knitters Company actively tried to prevent the entry of newcomers into the industry, probably signifying that profits were being squeezed. Felkin mentions the excellent technical progress of the industry down to Queen Anne's reign, but Professor Chambers sees little improvement in mechanization during our period.[15] Moreover, there was no change in institutional arrangements which militated against progress, that is the domestic production unit with its features of framework renting and the putting out system.

Cotton fustians had been manufactured in Lancashire from the early seventeenth century, but the yarn was too weak in places for knitting, and its unevenness made it difficult or impossible to loop it on to the needles. But the demand for cotton stockings increased and, because of their whiteness, they were preferred to silk. In 1730, a Nottinghamshire stockinger named Slater produced the first cotton hose. Professor Chambers has remarked that "... the local stockingers knew how to make cotton stockings on the stocking-frame as early as 1730, but it was not until the 1750s that Nottingham began to catch the fever of cotton-spinning...".[16] The desirability of dramatically increasing the productivity of spinners was as obvious in the cotton hosiery industry as it was in the wool textile industry. The idea of spinning by rollers occurred to John Wyatt in 1730, and a machine was made in 1733. Five years later, Lewis Paul secured a patent for roller-spinning. Although they co-operated, apparently nothing came of their endeavours: at least the few small factories in Birmingham and elsewhere using Paul's machinery during the forties proved unsuccessful. Another twenty years had to elapse before the problem was solved by James Hargreaves' spinning-jenny and Richard Arkwright's water-frame. Chambers reminds us that Arkwright ushered in the new factory age by building "ten massive spinning establishments in Nottinghamshire and Derbyshire alone between 1769 and 1784". But why did it take so long for roller-spinning to be perfected? Professor Wells thinks because "... it was not until about 1760 that the demand for more and better yarn grew really insistent". The beginning of the Industrial Revolution, Chambers entices us to believe, "... could well have happened thirty years earlier, at the time of the abortive venture of Lewis Paul, but the expansive market of the 1760s was then lacking".[17]

Metal Wares, Pottery and Paper

Many writers have commented on the vigorous growth of the metal trades, both in size and number, during the late seventeenth and early eighteenth century, especially from 1690 to the late 1720s. Throughout the country, and in particular around Birmingham and Sheffield and in London, master-craftsmen and domestic workers manufactured a large variety of products using iron, lead, copper, tin, and the alloys, brass and bronze. In the Tudor era, Birmingham was a small settlement whose economy was dominated by Warwickshire graziers and whose main purpose was to provide a market for agricultural produce. Its development between 1600 and 1660 is obscure but, over the next four decades, Birmingham and the surrounding Black Country rose to pre-eminence in the metal trades. As a result of the Act of Uniformity (1662), which made clergy use the Book of Common Prayer, many dissenters moved to Birmingham, a small town without charter and without guilds. The population of the area then grew rapidly, and new industries were established to make metal buttons, brass-ware and jewellery.[18]

By 1700, the variety of metal wares had become much enlarged, and included locks, keys, hinges, guns, swords, cane-heads, snuff-boxes, clocks, watches, brass toys, and all manner of artistic goods and hardware. Professor Court remarks on the considerable increase in Birmingham's production of guns, cutlery, and all articles of wrought iron, particularly over the years 1698 to 1711.[19] Exports of knives and hardware rose greatly after the African trade opened in 1698, and exports of copper-wares between 1710 and 1720 increased from 189 to 1,694 hundredweights. Professor Hamilton notes that the expansion of demand for metal wares after 1690 owed much "... to the creation of demand for artistic goods and the interruption of trade with France, which had been accustomed to supply these goods; the expansion of foreign trade; and the great developments in copper mining and the production of brass after 1690". He also assures us that "... *during the first quarter of the eighteenth century* the brass trades progressed very rapidly, so that when Defoe wrote in 1728 he considered it unnecessary to emphasize the importance of Birmingham wrought iron and brass manufacturers".[20] Are we to infer that progress became less rapid from the late twenties? Certainly Court and Hamilton report no significant changes during the second quarter of the eighteenth century.

It seems certain that the output of metal wares continued to rise and their quality to improve in the thirties and forties. But it is doubtful whether the flourishing state of producers (except for the notoriously exploited nailers) was maintained. On the assumption that high quality and therefore relatively expensive products were sold to the upper-middle and wealthy classes, we should expect the history of the silk industry to be some guide to the level of demand. Moreover, in those parts of the country suffering from agricultural depression, some families might well have seized any opportunity to join the ranks of unskilled metal workers. To the extent that this occurred, the higher output of some metal wares responded not to a more buoyant level of expenditure but to an over-supplied labour market. Of course, the profitability of this section of the economy was raised by military expenditure during the Austrian Succession War (1739–48), but in all probability the impact of this expenditure was felt mainly after 1744 when war was officially declared against France. Ramsey Muir has written of this conflict between Britain and France as having been "fought. . . in a strangely half-hearted and lackadaisical way". In any event, it appears the war brought only a temporary respite to the metal trades because, in 1752, a petition was delivered to Parliament stressing the poverty in which the great majority of Birmingham manufacturers found themselves.[21]

The cutlery and hardware trades in and around Sheffield responded disappointingly to important technical developments until after the middle of the eighteenth century. G.I.H. Lloyd reports that ". . . the pioneers in the steel manufacture were Samuel Shore and George Steer. The former was making blister steel by 1709, and the latter in 1719." Despite their efforts, output expanded slowly throughout the first half of the century. Nor apparently did the pace of advance quicken for many years after Benjamin Huntsman's invention of the crucible method of converting blister into cast steel in 1740 and, about the same time, Thomas Bolsover's invention of a silver-plating technique. Huntsman's invention was especially important because it enabled sharp, reliable metal-cutting tools to be made.[22] It is difficult to explain the delay in exploiting these inventions except by reference to the generally unfavourable economic climate of the time. The metal trades everywhere continued to be organized mainly on a domestic basis, and there was little movement towards the factory system. By the late fifties, however, the fortunes of metal manufacturers seem to have improved. We recall the much-quoted statement of Josiah Tucker (1757): "Almost every Master-Manufacturer hath a new Invention of his own, and is daily improving on those of others." Birmingham manufacturers began to adopt the method of silver-plating copper on a significant scale. And of course a new era was launched with the building of Matthew Boulton's Soho factory in 1762. As we shall see later, the history of the metal trades has some parallel in that of the copper- and tin-mining industries which experienced two waves of expansion, the first after 1690 and the second from the mid-eighteenth century.[23]

It is well known that, like the metal trades, the pottery industry is older than recorded history. Again, like the metal trades, it was widespread, and could be found in most areas where suitable clays were available. Some geographic specialization took place, and Staffordshire emerged as the leading centre in the seventeenth century. However, while the skills of metal workers improved markedly down the centuries, very little progress was made by potters. Theirs remained a desperately poor, peasant industry using equipment and working in establishments which, as late as 1600, were "so simple that primitive man would have found nothing strange about them".[24] This situation underwent an incredible transformation between 1600 and 1800, the main advances occurring between 1690 and the mid-1720s, and after 1760. The demand for better pottery increased after 1600 as the habit of drinking tea and coffee spread among the higher echelons of society. But the greatest stimulus to the industry during the seventeenth and early part of the eighteenth century was the importation of German and Dutch stoneware, Delft ware, and oriental porcelain.[25] From the first decades of the seventeenth century, some potters experimented with sand, clays and lead, and later with salt, so it became possible to produce by 1690 a whiter, more attractive pottery called Crouch ware. The latter had the advantages of being both ornamental and utilitarian.

The pottery industry benefited from major technical advances in the years after 1688. It is believed about that year the Saxon brothers, David and John Elders, arrived in England and taught English potters the glazing properties of salt. They also showed how production methods could be improved, and Staffordshire potters learned from them how to make ornamental red and black teapots. The quality of Crouch ware was raised and so, by the early eighteenth century, the industry was progressing well. The competitiveness of the British product was much enhanced when, in 1720, John Astbury discovered – or stole the secret of – a means of salt-glazing which significantly inreased the whiteness of stoneware. In the same year, he successfully experimented with calcinated flint as a whitening agent. Unfortunately, crushing the flints caused lung damage, often with fatal results, through the inhalation of silica dust. This problem was overcome by a painter, Thomas Benson, who introduced a flint-mill in 1726 and so enabled flints to be ground under water.[26]

Undoubtedly these technical developments paved the way for the larger volume of pottery sales on both home and oversea markets during our period. Again we do not deny that some further progress was made, probably the most important change occurring in 1730 when moulds were first used as a substitute for the potter's wheel. But the pace of technical advance in the British industry after the mid-twenties was insufficent to prevent foreign competition from presenting a new challenge in the late forties and fifties. R. Campbell wrote in 1747: The London potters "... . never will encourage an improvement in the Stone Ware. . . and I am of Opinion that those of Liverpool are not able to be at the expense of proper Experiments". And Dr. Johnson observed that " ... he could have vessels of silver of the same size as cheap as what were here [Derby] made of porcelain".[27] French and Dresden wares were becoming more elegant than Staffordshire stoneware (whose salt-glaze gave a pitted appearance), and consequently this branch of the industry faced a crisis by the late fifties. Josiah Wedgwood entered in his first Experiment Book (1759): "The demand for our goods is decreasing daily."[28] The pottery industry was of course revitalized by Enoch Booth and Wedgwood during the third quarter of the eighteenth century. Our period witnessed a temporary boom in sales, little technical advance, and no perceptible transition towards mass factory production.

Although the first paper-mill in England dates from the last years of the fifteenth century, the industry did not become firmly established until the late sixteenth and early seventeenth century.[29] Most of the country's paper requirements were satisfied by imports until the 1670s. The half century beginning in 1670 witnessed substantial headway in the English branch of the industry together with the development of the industry in Scotland and Ireland. Professor Coleman sees the last quarter of the seventeenth century as a turning point in the progress of the industry, and he believes the output of paper increased fourfold between 1710 and 1720 with the result that about two-thirds of England's consumption was domestically produced by the twenties. Two factors in particular stimulated the rapid growth of the industry after 1670. Many technical improvements led to a better product and, secondly, the industry received considerable protection from competing imports, especially those from France. Between 1678 and 1685, all major imports from France, including paper, were prohibited. During the war years, 1689 to 1697, and from 1701 to 1713, Anglo-French trade was at a very low ebb. The import duty on paper, which had been 5 per cent down to 1690, reached 15 per cent by 1700. In addition, all French goods were subject to a tariff of 25 per cent in 1692–3 and another 25 per cent in 1696–7. Owing to political pressures, these import duties were maintained after the Treaty of Utrecht in 1713.

Starting in the twenties, the paper industry fell on hard times with both output and imports stagnating until a turning point not readily discernible between 1735 and 1745. The weaker demand for paper and its reduced profitability were evidenced by the experience of at least seven Kentish paper-makers who between 1727 and 1753 either went bankrupt, failed, or left the industry. Many paper-mills which formerly had been fulling- and corn-mills reverted to their original uses or served some other purpose. The advance of this industry down to about 1720 was not clearly resumed until just before the middle of the eighteenth century, after which its output increased quite rapidly until about 1790. In concluding this chapter, we think it appropriate to quote Professor Coleman's tentative explanation of the trend of paper output between 1670 and 1790:

> The spread of the beating-engine may have contributed to the change (in the 1740s); but in general terms it is worth noting that the trends exhibited here, in paper-making, are reflected in many other aspects of the economy. The striking relationship between the import and export curves has its parallels in indices from other industries and branches of trade; the timing of change seems also to reflect, however dimly it may yet be seen, the probable course of population growth. In short, the upward movement of paper output just before the mid-century may well have been simply a reflection of the general setting into motion of the economy. This new movement followed a period of comparative stagnation which itself followed on the rapid and vigorous economic upsurge which marks the last decades of the seventeenth century, an outburst of activity in which the paper industry shared.[30]

Notes

1 Professor Davis in a private communication. P. Mathias, *The First Industrial Nation*, p.3.
2 W.G. Hoffmann, *British Industry, 1700–1950*, translated by W.O. Henderson and W.H. Chalmer, 1955, pp.18-19.

3 Above, chapter 2, pp.27, 31-2.
4 N.A Briscoe, op.cit., p.178, pamphlets quoted in footnote; T.S. Ashton, *Economic Fluctuations*, p.76. Also cf. "The worsted and coarse woollen goods could be produced at far greater speed and required far less skill and care, and wages were necessarily much lower (than in fine silk work). Distress began to creep into these inferior branches of the industry about the middle of the century." (J.D. Chambers, *Nottinghamshire in the Eighteenth Century*, p.292.)
5 Phyllis Deane, *The First Industrial Revolution*, p.53. Our italics. See also Ralph Davis, "English Foreign Trade, 1700-1774", pp.286, 288.
6 R.B. Westerfield, *Middlemen in English Business, 1660–1760*, p.32. (basing himself on W.R. Scott, op.cit.).
7 Deane and Cole, op.cit., pp.52-3; N.B. Harte, "The Rise and Protection of the English Linen Trade, 1690–1790", in N.B. Harte and K.G Ponting (eds.), *Textile History and Economic History*, 1973, pp.104, 107.
8 H. Hamilton, *The Industrial Revolution in Scotland*, 1932, p.6; "Economic Growth in Scotland, 1720–1770", *Scottish Journal of Political Economy*, 1959, p.87; *An Economic History of Scotland*, 1963, pp.142-5; N.B. Harte, op.cit., p.99.
9 Above p.61. A.P. Wadsworth and J. de L. Mann, *The Cotton Trade and Industrial Lancashire*, 1931 (reprinted 1965), pp.134-5.
10 S. Lilley, *Men, Machines and History*, 1965, p.99.
11 A.P. Wadsworth and J. de L. Mann, op.cit., pp.464-7; Edward Baines, *History of the Cotton Manufacture in Great Britain*, 1835, reprinted 1966, pp.116-17. And cf. "The (cotton) industry was also experiencing a period of expansion in the early sixties and had adopted Kay's fly-shuttle in the previous decade, so that the demand for yarn stimulated a search for quicker means of spinning." (Miss Mann, in Singer, Holmyard, Hall and Williams (eds.), *A History of Technology*, 1959, vol. IV, p.177.) Also see this chapter, p.66.
12 J.D. Chambers, "Vale of Trent", p.13, and *Nottinghamshire in the Eighteenth Century*, p.100; F.A. Wells, *The British Hosiery and Knitwear Industry, its History and Organization*, revised edition, 1972, p.49.
13 The machinery embodied "97,746 wheels, movements and parts. . . More than 300 women and children were working a 24-hour day of two shifts in 1724. . . (the mill's) successors in Derby and Stockport were a microcosm of the Industrial Revolution." (C.H. Wilson, op.cit., p.299.)
14 Deane and Cole, op.cit., pp.53-4.
15 J.D. Chambers, "Vale of Trent", pp.13-14, 59; *Nottinghamshire in the Eighteenth Century*, p.292; Lujo Brentano, *English Gilds*, 1870, reprinted 1963, clxxx; W. Felkin, *History of the Machine-Wrought Hosiery and Lace Manufactures*, p.72.
16 F.A. Wells, op.cit., p.54; J.D Chambers, *Population in Pre-Industrial England*, p.125.
17 J.D. Chambers, loc.cit.; F.A. Wells, loc.cit.
18 W.H.B. Court, *The Rise of Midland Industries, 1600-1838*, revised edition, 1953, pp.43-4, 70, 141-2; Henry Hamilton, *The English Brass and Copper Industries to 1800*, 1926, pp.124-5.
19 W H.B. Court, op.cit., p.145.
20 Henry Hamilton, op.cit., pp.138-9. Our italics.
21 Ramsey Muir, *The Expansion of Europe*, 1939, p.37; Henry Hamilton, op.cit., p.273.
22 G.I.H. Lloyd, *The Cutlery Trades*, 1913, p.74; R.E. Leader, *Sheffield in the Eighteenth Century*, 1901, p.70; W.K.V. Gale, *The British Iron and Steel Industry*,

reprinted 1967, p.36.
23 J. Tucker, *Instructions for Travellers*, 1757, p.21; H. Hamilton, op.cit., p.274. See below, chapter 5, pp.75-6.
24 J.L. and B. Hammond, *The Rise of Modern Industry*, ninth edition, 1966, p.164.
25 Eliza Meteyard, *The Life of Josiah Wedgwood*, 1865, vol. I, pp.107-8.
26 J.L. and B. Hammond, op.cit., pp.165-7; Eliza Meteyard, loc.cit.; T.K. Derry and T.I. Williams, *A Short History of Technology*, 1960, p.585.
27 R. Campbell, *The London Tradesman*, 1747, p.185. This and the Johnson quotation cited by H. Heaton in A.S. Turbeville (ed.), *Johnson's England*, 1933, reprinted 1952, vol. I, p.233.
28 Cited by Brian Trueman, *Josiah Wedgwood: An Eighteenth Century Entrepreneur*, unpublished M.A. thesis, University of Nottingham, 1960, p.46.
29 This and the next paragraphs are based on D.C. Coleman, *The British Paper Industry, 1495–1860*, especially pp.12, 23, 54-8, 64-7, 90 and 161.
30 ibid, p.175.

5 MINING, TRANSPORT AND BUILDING

> Nor did any major break-through in industrial productivity occur before the mid-eighteenth century, at least in strategic industries like metals and textiles. This awaited massive machinery, made of iron, and the massive water-powered textile mills of the 1770s; then Watt's rotary steam engine of the 1780s. . . Invention did not produce cumulative innovation on the same scale as it did after the mid-eighteenth century. (Peter Mathias)

> Each short stretch of road needed a separate (Turnpike) Act, and they were common enough after 1700. Yet progress was fractional. (Charles Wilson)[1]

The Extractive Industries

The outstanding feature of the extractive industries during our period was the slow pace of innovation. Their profitability was adversely affected by either a weakening demand, or more commonly rising costs, or both. The main reason for rising costs was of course the difficulty of draining mines. By the year 1700, the output of the mining industries depended to a large extent on the working of progressively deeper seams, and consequently the problem of drainage became more and more acute and widespread. It is well known that the copper-tin industry of Cornwall was persistently handicapped by the danger of flooding throughout the first half of the eighteenth century. But many collieries and lead mines were also operating below the water level. Two examples are especially noteworthy: in a Warwickshire colliery, five hundred horses were employed to raise water in buckets from the pit, and the rich lead mine at Llangynog was abandoned in 1730 due to flooding.[2] Yet by about that date, as we shall argue shortly, the Newcomen pumping-engine was known in most mining areas but apparently few were installed before the middle of the eighteenth century.

Our thesis is well supported by the history of the copper- and tin-mining industries. The output of tin in the early seventeenth century was about the same as four centuries previously. It fell markedly during the Civil Wars, but advanced sharply afterwards. From Elizabethan times, the production of copper and brass was controlled by two monopolies, the Mines Royal and the Mineral and Battery Works. Their monopoly rights were violated after 1640 until they were withdrawn under the Acts of 1689 and 1694. Mr. Hill has underlined the importance of the 1689 Act: "From 1689 ['the *annus mirabilis* of the rights of property', Professor Stone called it] freeholders could mine copper or lead on their own lands (or sub-let the mining rights). Hitherto mines believed to contain gold or silver could be opened and worked by the royal monopolists, without compensation." The response was immediate and dramatic: many new companies were formed to mine copper and tin, and there was a great expansion of copper-working activities together with the introduction of a tin-plate industry.[3]

In 1703 and 1704, Acts were passed which raised the tariff on imported tin-plate from 8d. to 5s.3d. per hundred (single sheets) and from 1s.4d. to 10s.6d. per hundred (double sheets). The new infant industry became established, though in a faltering fashion, behind this tariff wall designed to wrest the home market from German exporters. Domestic consumption was stagnant down to the middle of the eighteenth century and production grew only slowly as it replaced imports. No doubt the slow expansion of the tin-plate industry was a major factor accounting for the weak demand for tin which became evident during the second decade of the century. From 1717 the tin market was controlled mainly by London merchants who kept its price low until the late forties. Domestic consumption of copper and brass probably fell between 1725 and 1745. Although exports of copper and brass continued to boom over this period (as before), the prices of both copper and tin had fallen to very low levels and tin had become "almost unsaleable" by the late forties. The subsequent rise in the output of tin-plate and in the demand for tin was associated both with generally more buoyant markets for metal wares and also with "improvement in methods of preparing the sheeting for coating with molten tin which was made between 1745 and 1760". Indeed, tin-plate was being exported to Ireland, Spain and the North American colonies by the mid-fifties. Both the demand for and output of copper also expanded vigorously from the late forties.[4] The low profitability of the copper- and tin-mining industries and the weak home demand for these metals from the twenties (or before) to the late forties provide further evidence for the view expressed earlier that, over these years, the demand for metal wares was far from strong.[5]

Turning to the coal industry, we recall that coal was substituted for wood or charcoal as a fuel in one industry and after another from the mid-sixteenth century. This process was given a strong boost towards the end of the seventeenth century when the reverbatory furnace was developed for smelting copper, tin and lead. Obviously this technological break-through much reduced the cost of smelting these metals and thereby stimulated the demand for metal wares, which in turn stimulated the demand for coal. Ashton and Sykes have estimated that the output of coal increased from 2½ to 4¾ million tons between 1700 and 1750. It seems likely that the industry expanded more rapidly in the earlier than in the later part of this period. The shipment of coal to London rose by about 30 per cent between 1700/2 and 1723/5 but then scarcely changed at all, apart from fluctuations, down to 1748/50.[6] Since coal was used as a household fuel, we must suppose its output was influenced by changes in population. As we have discussed earlier, the evidence suggests a significant increase in population between 1690 and 1720 but little change at all from the late twenties to the late forties.[7] Presumably the demand for coal as a household fuel increased during the earlier period and then stabilized. At least this interpretation is consistent with the volume of sea-coal entering London. The weaker demand for metals and metal wares during the second quarter of the eighteenth century is another factor we should bear in mind. Admittedly larger quantities of coal were consumed after than before 1725 – in the metal trades, brewing, distilling, sugar-refining and so on. But we are concerned here as elsewhere with probable rates of growth and probable changes in profitability. The vigorous and profitable upsurge in the output of coal during the second half of the eighteenth century was associated with three main developments (apart from the general advance of the economy): lower inland transport costs, lower drainage costs, and a demand from ironmasters switching from charcoal to coke-smelting. But, as we shall contend in the following pages, substantial progress along these lines need not have waited until after the mid-century.

Deceleration in the mining industries was the outcome of either a weaker or more probably a slower growth of demand in final-product markets, and the evermore pressing drainage problem. Facing these twin threats to their profits, colliery owners and other mining entrepreneurs had every incentive during our period to reduce the high and rising cost of drainage. The first real technical break-through came in 1698 when Thomas Savery patented his "Miner's Friend", an engine using steam-power. The Savery engine proved unsatisfactory because so much pressure had to be generated that often boilers burst or steam escaped through the joints. Far more effective was the engine patented by Thomas Newcomen in 1708. D.S.L. Cardwell believes the Newcomen engine was possibly the greatest single advance in the whole history of mechanical power. Its drawbacks have been emphasized by historians, particularly its waste of fuel and its low power-weight ratio. But its merits at the time were significant. Except for the cylinder and one or two specialized components, it could be made and installed by local craftsmen with very little engineering ability. Most of the components did not need to be correctly aligned, and they were long-lasting. The engine was simple to operate and to repair, great advantages in an age short of technical know-how. It was usually reliable and completely safe. Furthermore, the argument that it wasted fuel should not be taken too seriously because poor quality, almost unsaleable coal could be burned in the boiler.[8]

It is probable that the first Newcomen engine was built at Dudley Castle in 1712. Professor Harris, whose estimates are the most recent, has calculated that about sixty engines were constructed between 1712 and 1733, and three hundred between 1734 and 1781. Unfortunately we have no estimate for the mid-century, but a number of writers have suggested few sales were made before the 1750s, and the upsurge in demand for them came afterwards. Professor Harris' research is consistent with the view that the Newcomen engine was adopted less rapidly after 1725/30 and then far more rapidly after 1750. The two areas from which demand was the strongest were the North-East with its rich coal deposits and Cornwall with its copper-tin mining industry. The demand for coal, especially for use in the process of smelting iron with coke, increased sharply after 1750, and therefore it comes as no surprise to learn that nearly seventy engines were in operation around Newcastle in 1767. Ten engines at most were being used in Cornwall as late as 1741 but, during the next thirty-six years, sixty were erected there. Admittedly the cost of shipping coal to Cornwall and the tax on coal used in atmospheric engines (lifted in 1741) cannot be lightly dismissed in considering the copper-tin industry. Nevertheless the manager of the Wheal Fortune tin mine, a Mr. Lemon, earned a considerable profit with the aid of the Newcomen engine he installed in 1720. Louis Moffitt reports: "Lancashire was well to the front in point of engineering skill; although prior to 1750 there were few steam engines in the north." And Professor Hamilton tells us that: "The first of these engines to be installed in Scotland was at Elphinstone colliery in Stirlingshire about 1720, and the second was at Edmonston in Midlothian, although their employment did not gain favour until the second half of the century. They were not introduced into Glasgow collieries until 1763." And no engines were employed in the Lanarkshire coal-fields before the sixties.[9]

We believe that many entrepreneurs during our period failed to purchase a Newcomen engine through either lack of initiative or unwillingness to undertake long-term investment owing to general economic uncertainty and declining profits. The Newcomen pumping device was largely perfected and serviceable by 1720, and knowledge of the invention was widespread by the early thirties at the latest. It is perhaps significant that the Derbyshire lead-mining industry which was using six engines in 1733 managed to escape the general economic deceleration of the Vale of Trent. "Lead", confesses Professor Chambers, "was the only section of heavy industry which had retained its seventeenth-century *elan*".[10] To conclude then, we think it remarkable that, despite the growing severity of the drainage problem, and despite the expiry of the patent on the atmospheric engine in 1733 and the great reduction by the 1730s in the price of cylinders and pipes (about 90 per cent in the case of brass cylinders from Coalbrookdale), there was apparently no boom in engine sales during our period.

The Iron Industry

An early hint of trouble for the iron industry can be seen in the Statute of 1558 which prohibited the felling of trees for smelting purposes within 14 miles of the coast or navigable river. During the sixteenth century, large quantities of timber were used for building houses and ships, for forging tools and machinery, and it was also consumed in many industrial processes. In some regions, the forest was cleared, the land enclosed and converted into arable or pasture. The gradual conversion of Britain from a wood – to a coal burning economy after the mid-sixteenth century failed to avert a timber crisis, the revenue requirements of the Tudor and early Stuart monarchs in particular resulting in considerable deforestation.

> The first two Stuarts greatly hastened the danger of an oak shortage by extending the exploitation of forests commenced by the Tudors. The practice of deriving revenue at the expense of the future oak supply must stand as the real forest policy of England from 1535 to 1660. The Civil Wars and the Interregnum were to give the *coup de grace* to England's forest plenty. The forces let loose during those

> twenty years destroyed whatever surplus was left after the previous royal exploitation and failure to check waste.[11]

Professor Nef believes the iron industry advanced rapidly from the mid-sixteenth century to about 1610, its output then stabilizing or possibly declining. Moreover, in his view, "... there could have been no substantial increase in English iron production between 1660 and 1720". This is hardly surprising, given deforestation and the timber demands of the industry. Dr. Clarkson advises us that "... well over a ton of charcoal was needed to smelt a ton of pig iron (the ratio was 3:2 in the Forest of Dean in the seventeenth century) and even greater quantities of wood were required to make that amount of charcoal". A number of attempts were made to use coal in the smelting of iron before the eighteenth century. Lord Dudley took out a patent as early as 1621, and his more famous son, Dud Dudley, in 1638. The latter claimed to have smelted some iron with coal in his *Metallum Martis* (1665). If the Dudleys chanced upon a successful method, the secret died with them. Few would dispute the opinion of Mr. Gale: "Thus, although by a favourable combination of circumstances Dudley may have made a bloom or two of usable wrought iron, he could never have succeeded in doing so consistently."[12]

Coalbrookdale in Shropshire had been a centre of the iron industry since the Tudor era but, in 1709 when Abraham Darby and his family settled there, the scarcity of fuel had brought activities virtually to a standstill. Since Darby had worked in the malt trade which had been using coke for over half a century, his discovery of a means of smelting iron with coke is more readily understandable but none the less historic. Despite this discovery, probably in 1709, and despite Newcomen's invention in 1708, the iron industry continued to be severely handicapped by the shortage of charcoal and the difficulty of obtaining sufficient all-year-round blast power. There were long delays in solving these problems. It was not until 1743 that Abraham Darby II became the first ironmaster to erect a Newcomen engine and thereby secure power, even in dry seasons. And the coke-smelting technique was little used as late as 1750. Admittedly it had to be improved, and it was suitable only for making cast iron and not wrought iron. Nevertheless, the apparent lack of interest for so long in Darby's spectacular achievement is extraordinary. The process was never subject to a patent, yet the first published reference to it did not appear until 1747.[13]

The iron industry suffered reverses in many regions in the decades before 1750. Even the Darby family went through a bad phase for a while after 1717.[14] Because of the timber shortage, two companies moved from Staffordshire and Cheshire to Furness in 1711. There followed seven years of expansion in this part of Cumberland, after which no real progress was made until a second period of expansion between 1746 and 1756. The Backbarrow Company of this region set up a furnace in the backwoods of Scotland at Invergarry, near Fort Augustus, in 1727, but the enterprise failed in 1736. The York Buildings Company established an ironworks in Abernethy in Strathspey about 1730, but this venture was wound up about 1739. Moving to North Wales, we are informed by Dr. Dodd that a Charles Lloyd who, having learned from Abraham Darby how to smelt iron with coke, acquired a furnace soon after 1717 at Bersham, near Wrexham in Denbighshire. But, "... Lloyd failed to make his furnace pay, and gave it up in 1726... Another furnace at Ruabon... was abandoned as a complete failure". The industry in the rest of Wales fared no better. According to E.N. Jones, "By 1740 a shortage of charcoal had subjected many of the smaller ironworks to misfortunes from the effects of which they never recovered." And for the ironmasters in the Vale of Trent, "... the seventeenth century lasted until 1750: herein lies one of the most potent causes of the long pause... from 1725, a pause, which, in the case of the iron industry, became a retreat".[15]

The plight of the industry between 1660 and 1760 is underlined by the tariff protection it pressed for and succeeded in obtaining. Despite strong opposition from hardware manufacturers, English ironmasters secured an increase in the tariff on Swedish iron in 1668. Cutlers were particularly active between 1731 and 1738 in attacking efforts to have local iron replace the imported product. A number of pamphlets were published in times of crisis between 1717 and 1750, and parliamentary committees received statements from interested parties during the 1730s.[16] In the face of vigorous and bitter opposition, ironmasters persuaded Parliament to save the industry from virtual extinction. Thus the import duty rose from ten shillings a ton in 1688 to nearly fifty shillings after 1759. With a landed price of considerably less than £10 a ton, the level of protection was high. Notwithstanding this assistance, it has been estimated that the output of English pig-iron was about 26,000 tons a year between 1625 and 1635, and in the 20,000 to 25,000 ton range during the 1720s. "The iron trade (in 1740)", wrote Scrivenor, "seemed dwindling into insignificance and contempt". We agree with Miss Deane's judgment: "The evidence suggests that the English iron industry in the first half of the eighteenth century was scattered, migratory, intermittent in operation and probably declining."[17]

We cannot disprove the view of Professor Flinn that the output of pig-iron increased from 1660 to 1760, and more rapidly after than before 1710. Much of his case rests on the number of new furnaces and forges that were built. But this activity is hardly surprising in an industry forced to move periodically as its fuel supplies gave out. He admits that against the new investment has to be set the units which went out of business, and here "information is less precise". Flinn's position has been strengthened by the research of Dr. Hyde who has estimated that output increased from some 25,000 tons in 1715/20 to some 30,000 tons in 1750. On this calculation the industry experienced a very slow growth in both percentage and quantitative terms between the early and mid-eighteenth century. Hyde also informs us that at least twenty-two new charcoal furnaces were built over 1720 to 1755, *but* twenty-five were closed down during the same period.[18] If we accept the most optimistic estimates, expansion of capacity was small indeed and, in any event, the industry was forced to locate in more remote areas in search of fuel, and generally away from areas where it was to prosper during the Industrial Revolution.

We have already noted the slow diffusion of Darby's technique. Because of Dr. Hyde's work, we cannot use to support our case the views of Professor Ashton and, in particular, suggest other ironmasters were ignorant of the new method. The speed with which Darby's discovery became known during our period may be irrelevant. Hyde has convincingly shown that, for most ironmasters at least, charcoal-smelting was cheaper than coke-smelting down to the middle of the eighteenth century. However, this in no way undermines the accepted view that charcoal costs had been driven to very high levels by the early years of the century. The subsequent trend was far from encouraging. To quote Hyde: "The variable costs of these (charcoal) furnaces increased *sharply* in the 1720s and then *slowly* declined in the 1730s and 1740s. . ." The coke-smelting technique spread after about 1760 and, once steam power replaced water power in the 1780s, the stage was set for the iron industry to play its role in the Industrial Revolution. According to Hyde, ironmasters used coal far more efficiently after the mid-century, and this must have been a major reason for the substitution of coke for charcoal in the smelting process. Given the scarcity of charcoal in our period, why did they wait so long?[19]

Inland Transport

The vigorous expansion of industrial and commercial activities after 1660 stimulated and was to some extent dependent on better transport facilities. The sea and rivers were the main highways, especially for long-distance traffic. Many river improvement acts were passed, a spate of them in the years 1662–5, 1697–1700, and 1719–21. Of course, some schemes were unsuccessful, and there were delays. Nevertheless, Mr. Hadfield's estimates are usually accepted, namely that about 685 miles of river were navigable in 1660 and about 1,160 miles in 1724. Professor Wilson has produced a map based on the work of T.S. Willan showing navigable sections of river in 1600–60 and additional stretches in 1724–7. But why do these writers choose the mid-twenties as a terminal date? The main reason seems to be that there is little progress worth reporting until the canal era of 1760–1830.[20]

Undoubtedly some attempts were made to facilitate commerce by inland waterways after 1730, the most successful probably being the extension of the Weaver to Nantwich in 1734, and the re-opening of the River Dee traffic (closed from the early years of the century) between Chester and the sea by the mid-forties. On the other hand, there seems to have been a lack of schemes and a number of long postponements. Following the passage of the River Douglas Act in 1720, a company was formed, but the plan was abandoned until 1733 and work did not begin until 1738. Because of slow progress, a new management took over the enterprise in 1740. Nothing came of the 1730 Act to make the Stroudwater navigable from Framilode to Stroud; a further Act was passed in 1759, but nothing was accomplished until the Stroudwater Canal was built between 1776 and 1779. After Derby was linked with the River Trent in 1721, Professor Chambers reports virtually no progress in the area until the canals of the late seventies. The first Duke of Bridgewater had wrestled with the problem of transporting coal the ten miles from his Worsley mine to Manchester, and obtained an Act in 1737 to improve the Worsley brook for this purpose. However, the plan never came to fruition, and nothing was achieved until the historic Act of 1759.[21] We do not deny that there was considerable opposition to navigation developments, from landowners who feared the loss of local markets, from farmers whose land might have been flooded, and from millers and others who used water power. But this opposition was not unique to the second quarter of the eighteenth century, nor is there evidence that it was stronger at this time. If it is argued that less scope existed for river improvement from the late twenties, we are still faced with the question of why the canal era was postponed.

The first British canal was built by John Trew between 1563 and 1565 when he constructed a three-mile artificial waterway, using a pound lock, to link Exeter and Topsham. The second and third canals were the Sankey Navigation, 1755–60, and the Worsley-Manchester Canal built for the (second) Duke of Bridgewater in 1759–61. Yet canals were technically feasible in the seventeenth century. Professor Nef mentions a tract of 1638 which advocated the building of canals to provide links between the main rivers in France. The merits of canals had been canvassed by, among others, Andrew Yarranton in the late seventeenth and Daniel Defoe in the early eighteenth century, both writers referring to the success of canals in France and the Low Countries and urging Britain to follow suit. Cole and Postgate remind us, "Birmingham suffered greatly from lack of transport facilities till the coming of the canals. This is largely why the Birmingham and Black Country manufacturer had to concentrate on the lighter wares, which could be carried by packhorses to the nearest convenient place where they could be taken further afield by river and sea." The Staffordshire potteries provide another example of a region and an industry hampered by high transport costs. Not only was pottery carried over long distances by packhorse but, after Astbury's discoveries of the 1720s, clay was imported from Devon and Cornwall. The need for cheap inland water transport must have been apparent well before 1760. H.L. Beales tells us that "Dean Tucker. . . opined that there were not many rivers naturally navigable in this country, and that 'the high Tolls or Duties laid upon' those that had been rendered navigable were 'a great check to Navigation' ". And to quote Professor Ashton: "At their best, English rivers could provide but a slow and expensive means of transport."[22]

However slow and expensive river transportation, the cost per mile of carrying goods by land was nearly always far greater: according to one estimate, the cost of hauling a ton of goods over twenty miles in 1750 might have doubled their price.[23] Most accounts indicate that only minimal progress, if any, was achieved in road improvement before the second half of the eighteenth century. Some historians believe that British roads deteriorated almost continuously after the departure of the Romans, and that the Statute of 1555 which transferred responsibility for road maintenance from the manor to the parish did not reverse the trend. Indeed, the increase in coach traffic during the seventeenth century played havoc with road surfaces. The first turnpike act was passed in 1663 and, even though parliamentary activity in this direction quickened after 1700, the total mileage turnpiked was low before the 1750s. Reference has often been made to the traveller from Scotland who, in 1739, encountered no turnpike before Grantham, 110 miles north of London. And the delay in news spreading of the 1745 rebellion underlined the poor state of communications. In any case, turnpiking a road did not necessarily result in a significantly wider or better surface. Arthur Young, for example, in his *Southern Counties Tour* (1768) encountered exceptionally a good turnpike: "As to all the rest, it is a prostitution of language to call them turnpikes."[24] Not only was the financial mismanagement of the turnpike trustees notorious but, especially in the thirties and forties, toll-gates and -houses were frequently attacked and sometimes destroyed by rioters, and the evasion of tolls was ignored or even condoned by the gentry.[25]

Very little real headway was made if we are to judge by the writings of many regional historians who dwell on the very bad state of roads and the failure to improve them. For the Vale of Trent, Professor Chambers sees improvement occurring under the stimulus of expanding regional trade down to 1725 when an act was passed for turnpiking a section of the Great North Road, but thereafter he finds activity at a low ebb until the Nottingham-Kettering road was turnpiked in 1753. There was no extension of the turnpike system in Lancashire, Cheshire and the Isle of Man between 1735 and 1750. Louis Moffitt reports slow progress in Lancashire to which only eleven acts applied before 1750. An important feature and cause of the stagnation of the North Wales economy in the period before 1750/60 was ". . . the state of the roads (which) made it impossible to reach a wide market except in districts fortunate enough to have seaports within easy call, and the seaports themselves were silting up from want of capital to keeping them open". Everywhere in Scotland roads have been described as being in an appalling state by 1750, and in most areas too poor for wheeled vehicles. In 1725, a petition was delivered to Parliament stressing the desperate condition of roads between Norwich and London but, given Arthur Young's complaints forty years later, it was of no avail. "As to Norfolk and her natural roads", wrote Young, ". . . all I have to remark is that I know not one mile of excellent road in the whole country". All this evidence is consistent with Dr. Albert's overall assessment: "However, turnpike activity fell off sharply in the 1730s and, although there was some recovery in the forties, turnpike activity did not increase substantially until 1750."[26]

Our case leads to no decisive verdict, but it does throw doubt on

Professor John's view that transport improvement continued unabated during the second quarter of the eighteenth century. He notes that between 1700 and 1750 about forty-six river improvement acts were passed, four-fifths of them between 1720 and 1740. We do not deny that the early and mid-twenties witnessed considerable activity in promoting waterway development: indeed, this is understandable after the many acts passed over 1719 to 1721. If, as we believe, the rate of progress was not maintained, the period of slackened effort began probably some time in the late twenties. We should also remember that some (many?) turnpike and river improvement acts became in the event merely declarations of hope. Despite the number of turnpike acts, nearly one hundred in the thirties and forties, the great majority of highways were in very poor condition for some time after the turnpike network became rapidly and widely extended after about 1750. We see no reason for rejecting Professor Jackman's conclusions that, in 1750, the highways were probably little or no better than in 1660, and they had become totally inadequate to cope with the transport needs of the country. Transport costs may well have been rising in the first half of the eighteenth century, thus confirming the impression that road and waterway improvements failed to keep pace with the growing needs of internal commerce. Westerfield, for example, has written: "In the first quarter of the eighteenth century there arose a river trade in coal from the mines of Lancashire and Yorkshire sufficient to supply the cities of the interior." And John has provided some statistical evidence: "Water carriage from London to Abington was stated to be 10s. a ton in 1719, 15s. in 1729, and 18s. in 1739, while the cost of land carriage between Birmingham, Leicester, Sheffield, and London is said to have doubled between 1700 and 1729." We do not wish to challenge his conclusion that ". . . the demand for transport tended to press upon supply". The worsening transport bottleneck was a prominent feature of the second quarter of the eighteenth century.[27]

Building and Finance

Apart from a few fluctuations, the building industry maintained a high level of activity for most of the period from 1660 to 1730. The speed with which London was rebuilt after the Great Fire of 1666, the more sturdy and healthy brick houses which replaced the previously largely wooden structures, the increasing use of brick as timber prices soared, and the erection of spacious and stylistic country homes are all well-known features of the late seventeenth and early eighteenth century. At times during the long conflict with France (1689–97 and 1701–13), the building industry suffered setbacks, the worst being from 1709 to 1712. Then, except for a short-lived and minor retreat after the collapse of the South Sea Bubble in 1720, the industry flourished down to 1730. It languished in the thirties and sank into a depression during the war years, 1739–48. In his report on the building trades in London, Sir John Summerson says they enjoyed boom conditions from 1715 to 1730, but the thirties and forties, particularly the period 1743–8, saw activity at a very low level. The publication of Wren's City plan in 1749 appears to have coincided with the end of the long building depression. The Common Council began to discuss "improvements" in 1753 and from 1760, when an act was passed for widening and improving City streets, the building trades entered a phase of vigorous expansion.[28]

This account based on Ashton and Summerson is supported by Professor Parry Lewis in his authoritative work on building cycles. In his view, the main factors affecting the fortunes of the industry were wars, demographic change, and interest rates. The Treaty of Utrecht in 1713 not only sparked off a high general level of demand but also meant that more labour and timber were available to the building trades. Consequently, activity increased from a low point in 1711 to a peak about 1724. "It was estimated", writes Lewis, ". . . that the number of new buildings erected in the metropolis in 1716–18 amounted to a fifth of the number standing in 1695". There might have been a minor trough in 1727, but Lewis assures us that the low activity of the early thirties is well documented. A ". . . halting, gentle, barely perceptible, rise (follows) until 1736, and then a decline to the second-lowest level of the century in 1744". The same author sees the late thirties as ". . . a time when much of London was literally falling down". No doubt, the rise of population down to the mid-twenties was a major expansionary influence, while the demographic reverses of the thirties and forties must have significantly reduced the demand for new dwellings. As we shall note shortly, interest rates were low and falling to the late thirties: while contributing to the earlier expansion, they failed to counteract the impact of the check to population growth on the building industry. The outbreak of war in Europe in 1739, Britain's entry into the conflict in 1744, the Jacobite rebellion in 1745, the poor harvests of 1740 and 1741, higher interest rates during the war period from 1739 to 1748, and the epidemics of 1740–2 and 1747–8, all these factors would largely account for the continued depression in the building industry down to 1748. The subsequent upswing was associated with the end of the war, rising population, and lower interest rates.[29]

Building was the largest single expense incurred by landowners in maintaining and developing their estates. Their building endeavours were impressive between 1575 and 1725 after which, as we mentioned earlier, there was comparatively little construction work in the countryside until 1760. The sixties witnessed the beginning of a new wave of expansion associated mainly with the quickening enclosure movement. Professor Chambers has emphasized the building implications of enclosure: "Enclosure by an Act of Parliament often implied the partial rebuilding of villages; new farmhouses – many of them on a massive scale – labourers' cottages, roads, gates, fences, and so on."[30] The flagging interest of landowners in enclosure and building during our period can be attributed to the low profitability of agriculture and the demographic pause.

The check to growth in the sectors of the British economy under consideration in this chapter might appear surprising in view of two powerful expansionary forces. We might have expected the high cost of draining mines, of smelting iron, and of inland transport to have stimulated cost-reducing long-term investments. In addition, falling interest rates must have been a strong factor influencing the expected profitability of a whole range of long-term investment projects. The legal maximum interest rate was progressively reduced from 10 to 8 per cent in 1625, then to 6 and 5 per cent in 1651 and 1714 respectively. The yield on long-term government stock ranged between 7 and 14 per cent in the 1690s, fell to 6–7 per cent between 1702 and 1714, then to 5 per cent in 1717, and to 4 per cent in 1727. For a time from the mid-thirties the yield was even below 3 per cent. The 1739–48 war saw the yield rise somewhat above 4 per cent before the 3 per cent Pelham conversion of 1757. Sir John Hicks has suggested one powerful factor which influenced the flow of funds to the government: "The sharp rise in the credit of the British government (marked by the fall in the rate of interest at which it could borrow, from 10 per cent under William III to 3 per cent under Walpole and Pelham) must surely be attributed, among other influences, to the fact that the 'Constitution' of 1689, once it was firmly established, gave to the British monarchy the continuity, and therefore the long-term credit, of a Republic."[31]

The capital market had become quite sophisticated by the early eighteenth century, and the differential yields on the Funds, mortgages, equities, bonds and bills reflected the usual considerations of liquidity and risk. Subject to the legal maximum interest rate, yields on paper titles usually moved sympathetically with the yield on long-term government stock. Time-series data support this assessment, and it is reasonable to assume arbitrage transactions kept yield differentials within bounds. Professor Ashton concludes that the yield on government stock "... is an accurate index of the supply of loanable funds at all levels". Unfortunately this statement omits the demand factor in the market equation. Falling interest rates indicate that the supply of loanable funds is outstripping the demand for them. They are consistent with both a rising supply and a falling demand.[32]

On Professor Ashton's authority, we can assert that "... the price of the Funds may be taken as an index of the supply of loans available to builders and contractors". During our period then they had access to plentiful finance at very attractive interest rates, but these strong inducements encountered a weak demand because, as we have seen, building activity declined in the thirties and slumped in the forties. Borrowing by industrial entrepreneurs might have been inhibited by the Bubble Act which effectively removed the safeguard of limited liability, and by the paucity of banking facilities outside London. We do not stress these deterrents owing to the popularity of the mortgage as an instrument of raising finance. The main obstacle to long-term investment was almost certainly a combination of ignorance, uncertainty, and pessimistic expectations of entrepreneurs. The very low interest rates which prevailed during the second quarter of the eighteenth century reflected in some measure a reluctance to borrow which, in turn, can be most readily explained by the general economic climate.[33]

The chief recipients of loanable funds in the private sector between 1725 and 1750 were merchants and landowners. Self-liquidating commercial bills and mortgages secured by the nation's greatest asset were the safest avenues for investment after the Funds. The increase in circulating capital in the form of commercial bills and other lines of short-term credit largely reflected some growth of international trade (though, as we have observed, this was not on an impressive scale) and also a larger output produced within a traditional industrial framework. Landowners must have welcomed cheap finance as they struggled to maintain ostentatious living standards and undertake mainly replacement investment. It seems that they were equally adverse to sinking long-term capital into agrarian and non-agrarian ventures. However, from the mid-eighteenth century, they became prominent not only in injecting massive doses of capital into their estates, but in exploiting their mineral resources and in promoting the infrastructure of the economy (e.g. turnpikes and canals). Commenting on the combination of very low interest rates and low turnpike activity in the 1730s and 1740s, Dr. Albert writes: "This may have been due in part to the continuing difficulties in agriculture and economic conditions generally unfavourable to long-term investment." Whatever the reasons, our period was characterized on the one hand by an urgent need to undertake capital projects, and on the other by historically ultra-cheap finance.[34]

Notes

1 Peter Mathias, *The First Industrial Nation*, pp.16-17; C.H. Wilson, op.cit., p.278.
2 John Rowe, *Cornwall in the Age of the Industrial Revolution*, 1953, pp.2, 7; D.S. Landes in H.J. Habakkuk and M. Postan (eds.), *The Cambridge Economic History of Europe*, 1965, vol. VI, p.326; John Lord, *Capital and Steam Power*, second edition, 1966, pp.24-5; A.H. Dodd, op.cit., p.22.
3 Deane and Cole, op.cit., p.60; Henry Hamilton, op.cit., p.68; John Rowe, loc.cit. Christopher Hill, op.cit., p.139.
4 Quotations from John Rowe, op.cit., pp.42, 43, 49. Other references are W.E. Minchington, *The British Tinplate Industry*, 1957, especially pp.12-15; Deane and Cole, op.cit., p.58.
5 Above, chapter 4, pp. 66-8.
6 T.S. Ashton and J. Sykes, *The Coal Industry in the Eighteenth Century*, 1929, p.14; and Appendix E (the latter being used by Mitchell and Deane, op.cit., p.112).
7 See above, chapter 3, pp.53-5.
8 D.S.L. Cardwell, *Steam Power in the Eighteenth Century*, 1963, pp.18, 23, 25-6; A. Wolf, *A History of Science, Technology, and Philosophy in the Eighteenth Century*, 1939, p.612; A.E. Musson and E. Robinson, "The Early Growth of Steam Power", *Economic History Review*, 1959, p.424.
9 J.R. Harris, "The Employment of Steam Power in the Eighteenth Century", *History*, 1967, pp. 138-42; H.W. Dickinson, *A Short History of the Steam Engine*, second edition 1963, pp.37, 43, 46, 48-9, 54-5; J. Rowe, op.cit., pp.7, 51; J. Lord, op.cit., pp.38-9; Paul Mantoux, *The Industrial Revolution in the Eighteenth Century*, reprinted 1961, p.357; L.W. Moffitt, *England on the Eve of the Industrial Revolution*, 1925, p.165; H. Hamilton, *Economic History of Scotland*, pp.188, 208.
10 J.D. Chambers, "Vale of Trent", pp.7,11; J.R. Harris, op.cit., pp.141-2.
11 J.N.L. Baker, "England in the Seventeenth Century", in H.C. Darby (ed.), *An Historical Geography of England before A.D. 1800*, 1936, p.395.
12 J.U. Nef, *The Rise of the British Coal Industry*, p.168; L.A. Clarkson, op.cit., p.87; W.K.V. Gale, op.cit., p.31.
13 J.P.M. Parnell, *Civil Engineering*, 1964/5, p. 275; C.H. Wilson, op.cit., p.199; M.W. Flinn, "Abraham Darby and the Coke-Smelting Process", *Economica*, 1959; Paul Mantoux, op.cit., p.299; Phyllis Deane, *The First Industrial Revolution*, p.104.
14 "Abraham Darby the first died in 1717, leaving a flourishing iron-foundry,

which his sons were too young to work and which was sold at a loss. In due course, the next generation of Darbys grew up in Coalbrookdale, and took up their father's trade of iron founding under the management of Abraham the second." (J.P.M. Parnell, loc.cit.

15 J.D. Marshall, *Furness and the Industrial Revolution*, 1958, p.28; H. Hamilton, *The Industrial Revolution in Scotland*, pp.151-3; A.H. Dodd, op.cit., p.23; E.N. Jones, *The Economic History of Wales*, 1928, p.48; J.D. Chambers, 'Vale of Trent", p.9.

16 G.L.H. Lloyd, op.cit., pp.71, 75; M.W. Flinn, "The Growth of the English Iron Industry, 1660–1760", *Economic History Review*, 1958, p.145.

17 R. Davis, "The Rise of Protection in England, 1689–1786", *Economic History Review*, 1966, p.315; H. Scrivenor, *History of the Iron Trade*, 1854 edition, p.56; Phyllis Deane, op.cit., pp.103-4.

18 C.K. Hyde, "The Adoption of Coke-Smelting by the British Iron Industry, 1709–1790", *Explorations in Economic History*, p.397; M.W. Flinn, loc.cit. Professor Flinn is right to warn us that ". . . estimates of total production cannot be more than wild guesses" (p.148). This qualification applies equally to the other estimates we have quoted.

19 C.K. Hyde, op.cit., pp.403-4 (our italics), and p.412.

20 E.C.R. Hadfield, *British Canals*, second edition, 1966, especially pp.23-6; T.S. Willan, *River Navigation in England*, new impression, 1964, especially pp.28-30; C.H. Wilson, op.cit., p.279.

21 T.S. Willan, op.cit., pp.49, 71; L.T.C. Rolt, *Inland Waterways of England*, 1950, pp.34-5, 39; J.D. Chambers, "Vale of Trent", p.11.

22 E.C.R. Hadfield, loc.cit.; J.U. Nef, op.cit., p.259; J.P.M. Parnell, op.cit., p.57; Mathias, op.cit., p.109; G.D.H. Cole and Raymond Postgate, *The Common People, 1746–1946*, fourth edition 1949, reprinted 1968, p.41; J.L. and B. Hammond, op.cit., p.168; H.L. Beales in A.S. Turbeville (ed.), *Johnson's England*, vol. I, p.15; T.S. Ashton, *The Industrial Revolution, 1760–1830*, 1948, p.46.

23 E.J. Hobsbawm, *Industry and Empire*, 1968, p.30.

24 ibid., pp.90, 101, 111-12, 248-51.

25 H.L. Beales, in A.S. Turbeville (ed.), op.cit., p.131. W.T. Jackman, *The Development of Transportation in Modern England*, second edition, 1962, p.72.

26 J.D. Chambers, "Vale of Trent", pp.11-12; T.W. Freeman, H.B. Rogers, R.H. Kinwig, *Lancashire, Cheshire and the Isle of Man*, 1966, p.60; L.W. Moffitt, op.cit., pp.98-9; A.H. Dodd, op.cit., p.25; H. Hamilton, *The Industrial Revolution in Scotland*, p.226; W.T. Jackman, op.cit., p.98; Arthur Young, *Southern Counties Tour*, 1768, p.251; W. Albert, *The Turnpike Road System in England, 1663–1840*, 1972, p.116.

27 A.H. John, "Agricultural Productivity and Economic Growth", in E.L. Jones (ed.), op.cit., pp.181-2; W.T. Jackman, op.cit., pp.101, 137; R B. Westerfield, op.cit., p.218.

28 T.S. Ashton, *Economic Fluctuations in England*, pp.91 ff; John Summerson, *Georgian London*, 1945, especially chapters VII and IX.

29 J. Parry Lewis, *Building Cycles and Britain's Growth*, 1965, pp.14-19.

30 C.H. Wilson, op.cit., p.256; J.D. Chambers, *Population in Pre-Industrial England*, p.124.

31 J.R. Hicks, *A Theory of Economic History*, 1969, p.94.

32 P.G.M. Dickson, *The Financial Revolution, 1688–1756*, 1967, pp.470, 472, 484; T.S. Ashton, *An Economic History of England*, p.28.

33 T.S. Ashton, *Economic Fluctuations*, p.88; Christopher Hill, op.cit., p.199; D.M. Joslin, "London Private Bankers, 1727–1785", *Economic History*

Review, 1954; T.S Ashton, *The Industrial Revolution*, p.97.

34 H.J. Habakkuk, "Economic Fluctuations of English Landowners in the Seventeenth and Eighteenth Centuries", *Explorations in Entrepreneurial History*, 1953; H.J. Habakkuk, "Essays in Bibliography and Criticism, The Eighteenth Century", *Economic History Review*, 1956; W. Albert, op.cit., pp.123-5.

6 CONCLUSIONS

> Pamphleteers writing in the 1740s, for example, used Sir William Petty's or Gregory King's estimates, made half a century or more before, to illustrate their assessments of the current economic situation. So little evidence did they see for economic growth that they were prepared to adopt calculations made in the 1670s or the 1690s to reflect the conditions of the 1740s. Population, prices and productivity could, they judged, fluctuate upwards as readily as downwards and there was no reason to expect them to go in one direction rather than the other. (Phillis Deane)[1]

We have not proved with certainty that the second quarter of the eighteenth century witnessed a deceleration of the British economy. But we believe the thesis has been substantiated beyond reasonable doubt; that is to say, nearly all the evidence together with plausible arguments and speculations point to the same conclusion. Many historians not directly concerned with the course of overall economic change in our period have advanced evidence and views which fit into the same general pattern. In our opinion, this pattern is best described as "deceleration" or "comparative stagnation", a slowing down in the growth and development of the economy. It is arguable that deceleration had begun well before the 1720s in the case of the iron industry and agriculture: the output of iron might well have changed little between the second quarter of the seventeenth century and the mid-eighteenth century, and the earlier agricultural revolution ended about 1690/1700. Nevertheless, the pace of advance on many fronts was impressive after 1660, and even more so after 1690.

Economic progress between 1660 and the early eighteenth century was itself a major cause of the subsequent deceleration. The rise in farm output reduced the profitability of agriculture. Improvements of the loom increased the productivity of weavers but created a shortage of yarn. The mining of deeper seams aggravated the drainage problem. The continued use of charcoal in smelting iron raised the cost of production to a level which threatened the viability of the industry. The rising volume of internal commerce put transport facilities under a greater and greater strain. These problems became more acute after 1725. The profitability of agriculture was very low in the thirties and forties. There was no change in the disequilibrium between the spinning and weaving sections of the textile and hosiery industries; indeed, if Kay's fly-shuttle had been adopted on any scale, the shortage of yarn would have been aggravated. And little or no headway was achieved in overcoming the bottlenecks in the mining, iron and transport industries.

While we do not deny that some advance both in quantitative and qualitative terms took place during our period, we cannot share Professor John's optimism in this respect. He is sure that ". . . the growing responsiveness of the home market encouraged manufacturers to be inventive and to direct production towards cheapness, as fashion ceased to be the prerogative of the rich". And he sees the buoyancy of the home market in ". . . cheap crockery, japanned wares, lace, Sheffield plate, the expansion of the copper and brass industries, the making of cheap mixed fabrics and their printing. . . Side by side with new products went qualitative changes in furniture and other articles."[2] We believe expenditure in directions significant for economic development was far from buoyant, and innovational activity, again in these directions, was far from encouraging.

The period under review might be described with only slight exaggeration as one of profitless prosperity. Low agricultural prices resulted in higher real incomes for most labourers, but some groups, for example in the hosiery and metal trades, appear to have suffered a fall in living standards by the forties and early fifties. Although the output of many secondary industries continued to increase after 1725, it should not be inferred that they responded to a high level of expenditure. Against the additional purchasing power generated by low food prices has to be set the effect on aggregate demand of a high leisure preference, a demographic pause, and the weight of taxation borne by the poor. Furthermore, on plausible assumptions regarding the income-elasticities of the poor and lower-middle class, we believe expenditure on non-food items other than gin, textiles, boots and shoes increased to only a modest extent. It seems probable that the output of the paper, silk hosiery and iron industries stagnated, while building activities were at a low level. There is good evidence of low profitability in many sectors of the economy. Supply outstripped demand for agricultural products, woollen and linen textiles, cheaper varieties of hosiery, and probably for metal wares. In addition to the agricultural sector, the iron, copper-tin mining and hosiery industries suffered a price-cost squeeze. And costs were high and probably rising in the extractive and iron industries and also in transport.

Low profitability inevitably undermined the confidence of entrepreneurs, increased their uncertainty and reduced their willingness to take risks. We have cited many examples of the slack pace of innovation: the slow enclosure movement, the failure to improve roads, the postponement of canal building, the likely slow adoption of the Newcomen engine, the long delay in substituting coal for wood in iron-smelting, the lack of significant mechanical improvements in the textile and hosiery industries. There was also little technical advance in the pottery and paper industries. In so far as the British economy expanded, it was mainly along traditional lines with little or no movement towards the factory system and mass consumption. The failure of Lombe's factory is especially significant, but we have also noted that the output of the textile and hosiery industries, and the metal trades increased within the established industrial framework. The transition towards mass consumption was hindered by the failure to reduce costs through innovation, by the check to population growth, and the rise in transport costs. The very slow improvement in the infrastructure of the economy despite the increase in commerce is an outstanding feature of the second quarter of the eighteenth century. Furthermore, by 1750, the iron and cotton textile industries had given no sign of their future role in catering for mass consumption needs.

In the face of low profitability and expected low rates of return on long-term investment in many areas of the economy, low and falling interest rates were largely ineffective in stimulating capital expenditure. Landowners were far more willing to mortgage their land to finance ostentatious living standards than to press ahead with enclosure. And industrial entrepreneurs were probably influenced more by their pessimistic expectations than by low borrowing costs. Moreover, for those with available finance, the Funds, mortages (mostly secured against land), and commerce must have appeared safer (and more liquid) assets than other forms of investment. Cheap money has sometimes been regarded as a sure sign of economic development during our period. In our view, low interest rates reflected in part a weak demand for loanable funds, and hence were yet another indicator of economic deceleration.

We believe the two most powerful forces inimical to economic development between 1725 and 1750 were low agricultural prices and demographic reverses. Similarly, the rising trends of agricultural prices and population from 1750/60 created an economic environment favourable to capital accumulation and risk-taking. Professor Habakkuk has underlined the significance of agricultural prices:

> The low or stationary agricultural prices of the earlier decades of the century had a depressing effect on agricultural investment and indirectly on the demand for industrial goods. The rising prices over most of the second half of the century stimulated agricultural investment and led to increased demand for industrial goods; they led not so much to a shift of income between the industrial and agricultural sectors as to an increase in the income of both.[3]

And we end with the intriguing speculation of Sir John Hicks:

> One cannot suppress the view that perhaps the whole Industrial Revolution of the last 200 years has been nothing else but a vast secular boom, largely induced by the unparalleled rise in population.[4]

Notes

1 Phyllis Deane, *The First Industrial Revolution*, p.11.
2 A.H. John, op.cit., pp.178-9.
3 H.J. Habakkuk, "Essays in Bibliography and Criticism: The Eighteenth Century", *Economic History Review*, 1956, pp.437-8, and cited by Deane and Cole, op.cit., p.90
4 J.R. Hicks, *Value and Capital*, 1939, p.302.

BIBLIOGRAPHY

The following alphabetical list contains all the principal works consulted.

Albert, W., *The Turnpike Road System in England, 1663–1840,* 1972.

Ashton, T.S., *An Economic History of England: The Eighteenth Century,* 1955.

Ashton, T.S., *Economic Fluctuations in England, 1700–1800,* 1959.

Ashton, T.S., *The Industrial Revolution, 1760–1830,* 1948.

Ashton, T.S., and Sykes, J., *The Coal Industry of the Eighteenth Century,* 1929.

Baines, Edward, *History of the Cotton Manufacture,* 1835.

Baker, J.N.L., "England in the Seventeenth Century", in Darby, H.C., (ed.), *An Historical Geography of England before A.D. 1800,* 1936.

Barnes, D.G., *A History of the English Corn Laws,* 1930.

Beveridge, Sir William, *Prices and Wages in England from the Twelfth to the Nineteenth Century,* vol. I, 1939.

Brentano, Lujo, *English Gilds,* 1870, reprinted 1963.

Briscoe, *The Economic Policy of Robert Walpole,* 1907.

Cardwell, D.S.L., *Steam Power in the Eighteenth Century,* 1963.

Chambers, J.D., "Enclosure and Labour Supply in the Industrial Revolution", *Economic History Review,* 1953.

Chambers, J.D., *Nottinghamshire in the Eighteenth Century,* second edition, 1966.

Chambers, J.D., *Population, Economy, and Society in Pre-Industrial England,* 1972.

Chambers, J.D., "Vale of Trent, 1670–1800", *Economic History Review,* 1957, Supplement no. 3.

Chambers, J.D., and Mingay, G.E., *The Agricultural Revolution, 1750–1880,* 1966.

Clark, Colin, *The Conditions of Economic Progress,* 1940.

Clarkson, L.A., *The Pre-Industrial Economy in England, 1500–1750,* 1971.

Coats, A.W., "Changing Attitudes to Labour in the Mid-Eighteenth Century", *Economic History Review,* 1958.

Cole, G.D.H.,and Postgate, Raymond, *The Common People, 1746–1946,* fourth edition, 1949, reprinted 1968.

Cole, W.A., and Deane, Phyllis, "The Growth of National Incomes", in Habakkuk, H.J., and Postan, M. (eds.), *The Cambridge Economic History of Europe,* vol. VI, 1965.

Coleman, D.C., "Naval Dockyards under the Later Stuarts", *Economic History Review,* 1953.

Coleman, D.C., *The British Paper Industry, 1485–1860,* 1958.

Court, W.H.B., *The Rise of Midland Industries, 1600–1845,* 1938, revised edition, 1953.

Davis, Dorothy, *Fairs, Shops and Supermarkets,* 1966.

Davis, Ralph, "English Foreign Trade, 1660–1700", *Economic History Review,* 1954.

Davis, Ralph, "English Foreign Trade, 1700–1774", *Economic History Review,* 1962.

Davis, Ralph, "Merchant Shipping in the Economy of the Late Seventeenth Century", *Economic History Review,* 1956.

Davis, Ralph, "The Rise of Protection in England, 1689–1786", *Economic History Review,* 1966.

Davis, Ralph, *The Rise of the English Shipping Industry in the Sevent Seventeenth and Eighteenth Centuries,* 1962.

Deane, Phyllis, *The First Industrial Revolution,* 1967.

Deane, Phyllis, "The Output of the British Woollen Industry in the Eighteenth Century", *Journal of Economic History,* 1957.

Deane, Phyllis, and Cole, W.A., *British Economic Growth, 1688–1959,* second edition, 1967.

Defoe, Daniel, *A Tour through England and Wales,* 1724–27, revised edition, 1962.

Derry, T.K., and Williams, T.I., *A Short History of Technology,* 1960.

Dickinson, H.W., *A Short History of the Steam Engine,* second edition, 1963.

Dickson, P.G.M., *The Financial Revolution. A Study in the Development of Public Credit, 1688–1756,* 1967.

Dodd, A.H., *The Industrial Revolution in North Wales,* second edition, 1951.

Dowell, Stephen, *History of Taxation,* 1884.

Ernle, Lord, *English Farming Past and Present,* 1936.

Felkin, W., *History of the Machine-Wrought Hosiery and Lace Manufactures,* 1867, centenary edition, 1967.

Fisher, F.J., "The Sixteenth and Seventeenth Centuries: The Dark Ages in English Economic History?", *Economica,* 1957.

Flinn, M.W., "Abraham Darby and the Coke-Smelting Process",

Economica, 1959.
Flinn, M.W., "The Growth of the English Iron Industry, 1660–1760", *Economic History Review*, 1958.
Freeman, T.W., Rogers, H.B., and Kinwig, R.H., *Lancashire, Cheshire and the Isle of Man*, 1966.
Gale, W.K.V., *The British Iron and Steel Industry*, reprinted 1967.
George, M.D., "Some Causes of the Increase of Population in the Eighteenth Century as Illustrated by London", *Economic Journal*, 1922.
Gilboy, E.W., *Wages in Eighteenth-Century England*, 1934.
Glass, D.V., and Eversley, D.E.C. (eds.), *Population in History*, 1965.
Gould, J.D., "Agricultural Fluctuations and the English Economy of the Eighteenth Century", *Journal of Economic History*, 1962.
Habakkuk, H.J., "Economic Fluctuations of English Landowners in the Seventeenth and Eighteenth Centuries", *Explorations in Entrepreneurial History*, 1953.
Habakkuk, H.J., "English Landownership, 1680–1740", *Economic History Review*, 1940.
Habakkuk, H.J., "Essays in Bibliography and Criticism: The Eighteenth Century", *Economic History Review*, 1956.
Hadfield, E.C.R., *British Canals*, second edition, 1966.
Haldane, A.R.B., *The Drove Roads of Scotland*, 1952.
Hamilton, H., *An Economic History of Scotland*, 1963.
Hamilton, H., "Economic Growth in Scotland, 1720-1770", *Scottish Journal of Political Economy*, 1959.
Hamilton, H., *The English Brass and Copper Industries to 1800*, 1926.
Hamilton, H., *The Industrial Revolution in Scotland*, 1932.
Hammond, J.L., and B., *The Rise of Modern Industry*, ninth edition, 1966.
Hammond, J.L., and B., *The Village Labourer*, fourth edition, 1926.
Handley, J.E., *Scottish Farming in the Eighteenth Century*, 1953.
Harris, J.R., "The Employment of Steam Power in the Eighteenth Century", *History*, 1967.
Harte, N.B., "The Rise and Protection of the English Linen Trade, 1690–1790", in Harte, N.B., and Ponting, K.G., editors, *Textile History and Economic History*, 1973.
Heaton, H., *Economic History of Europe*, revised edition, 1963.
Hertz, G.B., *The Old Colonial System*, 1905.
Hicks, Sir John, *A Theory of Economic History*, 1969.
Hill, Christopher, *Reformation to the Industrial Revolution*, 1967.

Hobsbawm, E.J., *Industry and Empire,* 1968.
Hoffmann, W.G., *British Industry, 1700–1950,* translated by Henderson, W.G., and Chalmer, W.H., 1955.
Hyde, C.K., "The Adoption of Coke-Smelting by the British Iron Industry, 1709–1790", *Explorations in Economic History,* 1973.
Hyde, F.E., *Liverpool and the Mersey,* 1971.
Innis, A.D., *Britain and Her Rivals in the Eighteenth Century, 1713–1789,* 1895.
Ippolito, R.A., "The Effect of the 'Agricultural Depression' on Industrial Demand in England: 1730–1750", *Economica,* 1975.
Jackman, W.T., *The Development of Transportation in Modern England,* 2 vols., 1916, second edition, 1962.
John, A.H., "The Course of Agricultural Change, 1660–1760", in Pressnell, L.S., editor, *Studies in the Industrial Revolution,* 1960.
Jones, E.L., editor, *Agriculture and Economic Growth in England, 1650–1815,* 1967.
Jones, E.L., and Mingay, G.E., editors, *Land, Labour and Population in the Industrial Revolution,* 1967.
Jones, E.N., *The Economic History of Wales,* 1928.
Joslin, D.M., "London Private Bankers, 1727–1785", *Economic History Review,* 1954.
Kalm, Peter, *Visit to England,* 1748.
Kelsall, R.K., *Wage Regulation under the State of Artificers,* 1938.
Kerridge, Eric, *The Agricultural Revolution,* 1967.
Laslett, T.P.R., *The World We Have Lost,* 1965.
Leader, R.E., *Sheffield in the Eighteenth Century,* 1901.
Lecky, W.E.H., *A History of England in the Eighteenth Century,* vol. II, 1878.
Lewis, J. Parry, *Building Cycles and Britain's Growth,* 1965.
Lilley, S., *Men, Machines and History,* 1965.
Lloyd, G.I.H., *The Cutlery Trades,* 1913.
Lord, John, *Capital and Steam Power,* second edition, 1966.
Macaulay, Lord, *History of England,* Firth's edition, vol. V., 1914.
Mantoux, P., *The Industrial Revolution in the Eighteenth Century,* 1928, revised edition, 1961.
Marshall, J.D., *Furness and the Industrial Revolution,* 1958.
Mathias, Peter, *The First Industrial Nation,* 1969.
Mathias, Peter, "Agriculture and the Brewing and Distilling Industries in the Eighteenth Century", *Economic History Review,* 1952.
Meteyard, Eliza, *The Life of Josiah Wedgwood,* vol. I, 1865.

Minchington, W.E., *The British Tinplate Industry,* 1957.
Mingay, G.E., *English Landed Society in the Eighteenth Century,* 1963.
Mingay, G.E., "The Agricultural Depression, 1730–1750", *Economic History Review,* 1956.
Mingay, G.E., "The 'Agricultural Revolution' in British History", *Agricultural History,* 1963.
Mingay, G.E., "The Size of Farms in the Eighteenth Century", *Economic History Review,* 1962.
Mitchell, B.R., and Deane, Phyllis, *Abstract of British Historical Statistics,* 1962.
Moffitt, L.W., *England on the Eve of the Industrial Revolution,* 1925.
Muir, Ramsey, *The Expansion of Europe,* 1939.
Musson, A.E., and Robinson, E., "The Early Growth of Steampower", *Economic History Review,* 1959.
Nef, J.U., "The Progress of Technology and Growth of Large-Scale Industry in Great Britain, 1540–1640", *Economic History Review,* 1934.
Nef, J.U., *The Rise of the British Coal Industry,* 1932, second impression, vol. I, 1966.
Nef, J.U., *War and Human Progress,* 1950.
Parker, R.A.C., "Coke of Norfolk and the Agrarian Revolution", *Economic History Review,* 1955.
Parnell, J.P.M., *Civil Engineering,* 1964.
Pawson, H.C., *Robert Bakewell,* 1957.
Plumb, J.H., *Men and Places, 1966.*
Riches, Naomi, *The Agricultural Revolution in Norfolk,* 1937.
Rogers, J. Thorold, *Six Centuries of Work and Wages,* 1909.
Rolt, L.T.C., *Inland Waterways of England,* 1950.
Rowe, John, *Cornwall in the Age of the Industrial Revolution,* 1953.
Schultz, T.W., *The Economic Organization of Agriculture,* 1953.
Scott, W.R., *The Constitution and Finance of English, Scottish and Irish Joint Stock Companies to 1720,* vol. II, 1911.
Scrivenor, H., *History of the Iron Trade,* 1854.
Singer, Holmyard, Hall and Williams, editors, *A History of Technology,* vol. IV, 1959.
Slicher van Bath, B.H., *The Agrarian History of Western Europe, 500–1850 A.D.,* 1963.
Smith, Adam, *The Wealth of Nations,* vol. I, 1776.
Summerson, Sir John, *Georgian London,* 1945.
Tooke, Thomas, and Newmarch, W.;, *A History of Prices,* 1838,

reprinted 1928.
Trevelyan, G.M., *England Under Queen Anne,* vol. I (Blenheim), 1930.
Trow-Smith, R., *English Husbandry from the Earliest Times to the Present Day,* 1950.
Trueman, Brian, *Josiah Wedgwood: An Eighteenth-Century Entrepreneur,* unpublished M.A. thesis, University of Nottingham, 1960.
Tucker, G.S.L., "English Pre-Industrial Population Trends", *Economic History Review,* 1963.
Tucker, J., *Instructions for Travellers,* 1757.
Turbeville, A.S., editor, *Johnson's England,* 1933, reprinted 1952.
Wadsworth, A.P., and Mann, J. de L., *The Cotton Trade and Industrial Lancashire,* 1931, reprinted 1965.
Wells, F.A., *The British Hosiery and Knitwear Industry, its History and Organization,* revised edition, 1972.
Westerfield, R.B., *Middlemen in English Business, particularly between 1660 and 1760,* 1915.
Willan, T.S., *River Navigation in England,* new impression, 1964.
Williams, E.N., *Life in Georgian England,* 1962.
Wilson, C.H., *England's Apprenticeship, 1603–1763,* 1965.
Wolf, A., *A History of Science, Technology, and Philosophy in the Eighteenth Century,* 1939.
Young, Arthur, *Eastern Tour,* vol. IV, 1771.
Young Arthur, *Political Arithmetic,* 1774.
Young, Arthur, *Rural Economy,* 1770.
Young, Arthur, *Southern Counties Tour,* 1768.

INDEX

For Product Safety Concerns and Information please contact our EU representative GPSR@taylorandfrancis.com
Taylor & Francis Verlag GmbH, Kaufingerstraße 24, 80331 München, Germany

www.ingramcontent.com/pod-product-compliance
Ingram Content Group UK Ltd.
Pitfield, Milton Keynes, MK11 3LW, UK
UKHW020208200926
475702UK00004B/668
* 9 7 8 1 0 4 1 2 7 9 2 3 5 *